The Lord
Is My Shepherd
and He Knows
I'm Gay

The Lord Is My Shepherd and He Knows I'm Gay

The Autobiography of the Rev. Troy D. Perry

As told to Charles L. Lucas

With a Foreword by Mrs. Edith Perry

Nash Publishing, Los Angeles

To those who have come with me to freely worship God, to stand unashamed at his altar, to know that we are gay and we are proud, to the congregations of Metropolitan Community Churches everywhere, to the growing ministry, to those who work with me, to those who have loved with me, to those original twelve who were at my first service in my home, and to the members of my family who have stood by me with unquestioning loyalty, I dedicate this book.

Foreword
by Mrs. Edith Allen Perry

If the doctor had told me, when Troy was born, that he was a homosexual—that he'd grow up to be one—I couldn't have loved him any less than I did, nor than I do now, nor any less than I love my other sons. And I've got four others. I'm proud of them all. They're all beautiful. Everybody tells me, when they see me with my sons, "My, what a nice looking bunch of boys you've got." They've all got so much of their father in them. People tell me that Troy looks like me. But I don't think so. I think they all favor their father. Anyone who sees their father's picture says that. He was a very distinguished, beautiful person. He was tall—as all my boys are—and well built, just like Troy, and like all of them.

When I was younger I didn't know anything at all about the homosexual way of life. Oh, I knew there was such a thing, but it never crossed my mind. I guess I was just never aware of it. I never recognized any sign of it—not really until

Troy. I had a very traditional reaction. I guess I thought "they" were all very soft and effeminate, rather like girls. That was my attitude.

But then homosexuality hit close to home. And when it did, and I found out about it, it like to have knocked me off my feet. It really was a revelation to me. I just didn't believe it. I couldn't.

I've learned so much from all that has happened. And now I know I'm a better Christian for having done so. I've seen the hard life that some have lived. I've seen some of the despair. And I've seen the hope, and the great energy that so many of my friends in the homosexual community have. I really think that the majority of them are so creative, so productive and so kind. The militants are fighting for their rights. They'd like to have me refer to the community as the gay community. And that's fine with me.

People ask me how I feel now about all that's happened. Well, the way I feel about it is this: Why should anyone live in a half world? Why should my son have to live that way? When Troy stood up to be counted with his gay brothers and sisters, and when he found his mission in this life, I figured that he was doing what he knew in his own mind was right. And I'm with him all the way. No one should live in a miserable world of shadows and be threatened with ruin and exposure. People, parents, children—no one should have to live that way.

I can't understand any mother that would turn her back on her children because they are homosexuals. It's hard to stand by them at first, and hard not to feel ashamed, because at first it's hard for them not to feel ashamed. But that shame is just being afraid of what others may say or think. And that's just plain silly, when it comes down to it. But if you accept them, and they accept themselves, then you can really learn the true meaning of love and family. I know. I did.

I couldn't feel a lot of things back then, when Troy was going through all of his struggle. In our background, everything was a sin. And it surely took a lot of thinking and praying to really realize that many of the old strict ways in which we were raised just aren't what it's all about. The real sins are hate and being inhuman to each other. That's how we all sin against the homosexuals. I'm glad that I've been able to discard that attitude in my life. I've met the nicest people that I've ever met in my life as a result of Troy's work. And I know that all of these men and women are just as deeply involved with God as any churchgoers could ever be. And I know my other sons feel the same way, and so do their families. We all know that Troy, like everyone else, must make his own way, no matter what. And that's just what he's doing.

We all want to end all of the bigotry and hatred, and the feeling that homosexual love is a sin. When that feeling gives way a little, then the feelings of having to be ashamed and of having to feel guilty and bad begin to go as well. Then these people can live happy and productive lives. I know. I've seen it happen right before my eyes. I've been a part of it. And it is a revelation. I hope it will be for others, too. That's why I'm glad Troy has chosen this time to tell his story.

The Lord
Is My Shepherd
and He Knows
I'm Gay

Introduction
by Troy D. Perry

One thing is sure. We homosexuals must all learn to rid ourselves of the sense of shame that we have been conditioned to accept from the heterosexual world. Such shame is no longer acceptable to any of us. How could we go on being ashamed of something that God created? Yes, God created homosexuals and homosexuality. It exists throughout history, and all over the world. We homosexuals number in the millions here in the United States alone. We must rid ourselves once and for all of the sense of shame I speak of. It comes, I think, through a sense of being alone. I'm sure that all homosexuals feel alone—often desperately alone—for long stretches of time. I know I did. And, being alone, being lonely, gives anyone a sense of solitary isolation. That is what has made us all vulnerable to the oppressive nature of the heterosexual world. I'm pretty sure that that world is not in as great a majority as it likes to think.

I am a minister of the Gospel. I have been licensed and ordained. I have finally found my mission in this life. And I am a homosexual, a happy homosexual.

For much of my life I carried the loads of guilt and shame that lead all homosexuals through a soul-wrenching and miserable wilderness. It was a challenging trial to learn self-acceptance. It was also a beautiful trial. I can say that as I look back on it. Why? Because, in accepting myself, I had to learn to accept others, all types of others, all types of homosexuals. I had been taught in my Southern schooling, and in my rigid Pentecostal church background that all of what I've grown to accept and love is evil and an abomination to God and man. I know now that it isn't. The opposite is the case.

I learned the truth when I finally found that I was really homosexual; when I began to ignore a feeling of furtive looks and restless airs, I knew that I was an instinctive rebel. Most homosexuals are. It is one of our basic attractions.

When I recognized the feminine pretensions of some of my fellow homosexuals, I recall seeing them as something of a novelty, a disguise, a kind of dandyism that earlier, sometimes repelled and frightened me. I thought that the obvious homosexuals were like sinister clowns exaggerating their own sense of novelty and aggressively putting others on; I wondered why they wanted to rock the boat. Why did they want to constantly irritate the established heterosexual society? They only attracted persecution and scandal. What I didn't know was that such gay young men with feminine airs were paving the way for the sexual revolution—the gay revolution—in which we are now so totally involved. As victims of society's injustice toward homosexuals, they could not be ignored. They are among society's wicked heroes.

At one time in my life I, too, felt that such obvious "fag" types were a threat and should probably be destroyed. One could see them only in secret and in darkness. Now I know that they are sons of our society—they are God's own children. As such, I have grown to love and embrace them. For deep down I know that in my own way I am as much a homosexual as they are. I have come to know that homosexuals come in every color, shape, size, age, religion, political stripe, and background. I know that intolerance is an enemy of mine just as it is an enemy of God's. I know that people are intolerant of those—the "they's"—of the world, and a part of my mission is to eliminate that attitude of "they." I have learned that man is alone everywhere, especially homosexuals. Now that we know this we can take comfort in it and band together. We have learned the true meaning of hypocrisy. In most organized religions hypocrisy seems to be a basic requirement for active membership. This hypocrisy makes all of us contemplate horror—man's own inhumanity to man. Most of us endure hypocrisy or the threat of it. We have allowed ourselves to become the disenfranchised. We are the butt of jokes, the last social minority to tolerate such put-downs. Only in 1968 did we really begin to fight back. The fight is lead by only a tiny fraction of our numbers, and I am proud to be in the vanguard.

The religious feelings of these, my people, are very deep, as has often been their misery and their sense of hopelessness. But most organized religions have been no more helpful to us than an empty well, to which we have all returned again and again in some kind of forlorn spirit of hope. We who committed ourselves to a homosexual existence grew gradually to accept a feeling that God did not care about us. That feeling served to place our real spiritual needs under a powerful and almost lethal anesthetic. It took a violent shock as powerful as a bolt of lightning to reveal to me this disgraceful condition arising from our own sense of solitude.

What set me on my course? Carlos, a young, handsome, dark-complexioned man, a Chicano with haunting eyes and a velvet smooth skin, who became a very close friend of mine. We were both "out" in the gay scene. That was in the spring of 1968. We had been attracted to each other. We scored. That is we really made the scene. And out of it we became really close friends and companions. We ran around a lot together. We heard of a really groovy new bar called The Patch that was going strong down in Wilmington. It was run by one of the most courageous and personable men I've ever met. His name was Lee Glaze, and he'd run bars in the Long Beach area. The local paper there had done a story on him called, "A Conversation With A Queen." Lee had his own personal civil rights movement going. His attitude was that anybody who got arrested in his bar would be taken care of. Lee would put up bail, pay the lawyers, and fight the case. And that's just the way it worked out.

The Patch was very well run. It was the first gay dance bar I was in. The music was fast and wild, and the guys all danced. The bar was so popular that I thought the crowds would push the walls out. It was the same every night of the week. To control crowds, Lee charged an admission, but it didn't keep anybody out. More people came. Lines of people waiting to enter formed around the block.

The bar was located in a fairly conservative neighborhood, and the local PTA decided to picket it. They did, and we thought that was wild. Well, we felt our oats, too, so two weeks later we went and picketed the PTA.

The next move came from the Alcoholic Beverages Control Commission (the ABC) and from the local police. They checked the bar to see if it was a public nuisance. It is if there are infractions of the law, such as minor's being served, or if any lewd or lascivious conduct takes place.

Carlos and I were there one night, and he went to the bar and bought us each a beer, came back to our table, and started to sit down. A fellow in plain clothes walked up to him, flashed his badge, and said, "Come outside with me!"

I said, "Do you mean me, both of us, or just who are you talking to?"

The officer said, "No, I'm not talking to you, I'm talking to him." And he pointed to Carlos.

They also took another friend of ours, a kid named Bill.

Outside, our friends were charged with lewd conduct, handcuffed, frisked, and hauled off to jail.

We moved fast. Some of us went right down to jail. Now this was about eleven o'clock at night. I knew that Carlos hadn't done anything. He hadn't broken any law, and I'm convinced of that to this day. But it took me until 5:30 in the morning to get Carlos released. It was all due to delaying tactics by the police. The booking procedure, the mugging, the fingerprinting, just took hours. It was just part of the usual harassment.

When I did finally see him, I could tell that he was more shook up than I was. And I was really upset. I took him home with me. I wanted him to get cleaned up, pulled together, and have something to eat. And, we'd plan what we were going to do.

Carlos said, "You know something? I've never been arrested before for anything in my life! Never! And I'm twenty-six now. The police there kept talking to me in Spanish and telling me that they were going to call my employer and tell him all about me. You know, Troy, I've learned one thing from this experience, nobody likes a queer. That guy will probably call my employer."

"Now come on Carlos, get off that trip right now. People do care. He won't do that. He's just trying to bluff you. Putting you down that way he probably thinks he's less of a queer than you are."

But Carlos wouldn't accept that. "I'm not so sure. But, look, Troy, be a realist, people really don't care. Nobody likes a homosexual."

"Well, Carlos, even if people don't, I'm still convinced that God does."

Well, Carlos just laughed bitterly, and said, "Oh, come on, Troy, God doesn't care about me. I even went to my minister, and I told him I was a homosexual. Do you know what he told me? He said that I couldn't be a homosexual and a Christian too. No, Troy! God doesn't care about me!" With that he turned and left.

When he left I felt the weight of his disaster upon me. I had made my way back to God enough, and I was still Pentecostal enough that I knew I could talk to God. So I knelt down and said, "All right, God, if it's Your will, if You want to see a church started as an outreach into our community, You just let me know when." And that still small voice in the mind's ear just let me know—*now!* And I took out an ad in *The Advocate,* and announced the first services.

I knew that the church I founded would be open to all, that its doors would be open to all, but especially to those who had been shunned and turned away by other sects, sects that have steadily refused to come to grips with the homosexual factor of the human condition.

The course would not be easy. I knew that we would all have to struggle as Christ did in the wilderness. I was sure that we would be tried in the balance, and I knew that we would *not* be found wanting.

To accomplish this mission I would have to reveal my own personal agony and search, and share my own ecstasy. I would expose my soul, and in so doing, I would be lifted up. So it has been. The campaign is clearly mapped out. The battles have just begun, but the war will be won—the war that will see us as shameless equals in the eyes of man, as well as the eyes of God.

This is the story of how I came through my own personal wilderness to the oasis in God's garden where I have begun to make my own vision a reality.

Mine is a triumph over bigotry, agony, loneliness and repudiation. I refused to lead a double life. I learned total honesty and self-acceptance. I have known for a long time now that the Lord really is my shepherd and He really does know I'm gay and He loves and guides me every day in every way.

I hope my story will serve to help others to a more honest acceptance of us and of themselves.

Chapter One
In The Beginning

I was lucky. So were my brothers. We were all conceived and born because our parents really loved each other. They expressed that love in the passion of a lustful sexual embrace, the currency of affection that passes on from one generation to the next. They were raised that way. So were we. For most of our family that cycle goes on without interruption. For me it has been different. I have an insight into my own beginnings that defies natural laws. For me that backward glance to first impressions goes back into the nameless universe of time. No, I don't recall where and when my soul began. I have an awareness of its existence down through the ages. When I stare into the beginnings of my soul I know that I feel the force of the cosmos and the infinity of God. That infinity is with me always, like a real physical presence. It is like knowing you have faith and belief. If you have that you are truly blessed. If you don't, your soul languishes in poverty.

One thing is certain about me! I feel that I have a total sense memory that predates my birth by a good long time. It's like being a seedling soul in two parts, your mother's and your father's genes. I have an awareness of having been a seedling—a physical presence in my father's sperm and in my mother's ovum before they united.

Now I know that I'm opening Pandora's box when I tell you that I'm sure that homosexuality is preordained. I think a lot more work has to be done in this whole field, but I am firmly convinced that much of what we are comes to us through our genes. I know that many people will throw up their hands in horror and say: "Why, where could you get such an idea? Where's your proof? Where's the data to support your stand? Where are your experiments? And, what theological reasoning or anything else could support such an idea?" Well, I'll just draw a blank. I just believe it, that's all. But you know, I read about a professor at the University of California who is conducting experiments along that very line. The rest of the people can wait for him. But not me. I'm sure. I'm going to go right on and believe it.

Sometimes I think it's just like catching the brass ring on the merry-go-round. I guess if you follow the law of averages, those who catch the brass ring turn out to be homosexuals. Well, I caught the brass ring. And, I'm sure that homosexuality was in my genes, and in my soul, from the very beginning.

So, this merry-go-round, this carrousel turns, as a child's kaleidoscope revolves, changing images constantly. So do I reflect upon my own beginnings. I've pondered my many beginnings many, many times.

But the images that come first to mind are the physical ones. It isn't easy to recall. But I can actually remember further back in time than the dilation of my own mother's body, and her forcing me from her warmth into the cold bright light.

Further back, I remember when I rested in my father's loins. It is really a sense memory of a kind of physical presence. I was only one with millions of would-be brothers. I, alone, survived. I was content. I had won the brass ring. My father's contentment was of a different sort. With an outburst of energy and emotion, he cast me forth into the sanctuary of my mother's belly. I felt forsaken by my father. The loss of him saddened me. But that period of mourning was only momentary. I fulfilled myself in the uniting, and in becoming a new life for this world. As I grew I explored my new environment, this thing called a woman's body—my dwelling place for those nine long months. This body nurtured me, cared for me, warmed and protected me. In time this body, too, evicted me in a wrenching burst of incredible and miraculous energy. Twice I had been thrust out of the temple of human flesh, a source of mystery and fascination for me. Would I ever really permit myself to trust the temple of human flesh again? Never completely.

That was on July 27, 1940. The place was Tallahassee, Florida, the state capital. Consider the setting into which I was born. The capital city is only thirty miles from the Georgia line. And one thing that hits you right in the face is that when you enter Tallahassee, you know it's a Southern town. But it isn't like most other Southern towns. There's an air of live-and-let-live about it. At least there was while I was around. There had to be. I think Florida is one of the most progressive of all the Southern states. Tallahassee reflects that. As far as race relations go, they've never had any of the major riots like those that have plagued Miami, Fort Lauderdale and other areas of Florida. There is friction, but I don't know of any really big difficulties. I must say that I've been away, so I haven't assessed the racial climate today. It may have changed. Everything does. That old carrousel does keep on turning. But the point is that when the federal government ordered school integration, Florida integrated. Period. There were no troops called out. The people really accepted the inevitable. It was a big change. Lots of them didn't really like it. But they did it. Maybe there's an attitude of fatalism there. But it is strange. Tallahassee was the only Southern capital that was never captured during the Confederate War. It capitulated in the Order of General Surrender. Still, the Union soldiers didn't come in for about two months. Why not? Well, Tallahassee is up in the panhandle of Florida, right out in the middle of nowhere. It was hard to get to then, and it still is. I don't think any Union troops were excited about having to move into Tallahassee.

People up in that neck of the woods are pretty settled in. They're set in their ways. They work hard. Most of them farm or have small business concerns. You can see that the atmosphere for learning there wasn't really geared to a lengthy study of metaphysics or to any really deep intellectual level. There are prejudices. I suppose it seems contradictory to say that. The prejudices have been traditional. Many have been handed down for generations without anyone bothering to really think about them, to sort them all out. It's that way about homosexuality there. True, the laws have changed. But a new effort is being made to tighten them up. I feared exposure there of my homosexuality. When I was a young married minister there, a real wave of persecution occurred. And persecution does alienate you and create a climate of fear and terror that can destroy you.

I think the important thing now is my general feeling, my first impressions—those senses of the physical nature of my world. I recall the sights and sounds of my world. These images expanded every day. I remember tastes, smells, a sense of touch. And I was always curious about everything. I still am. I wondered how people grew up, and why did grownups really do the things they did. Why was everyone so different? Why did it rain? And what was rain anyway? Why was it cold in winter? Now, only fleeting impressions of these questions remain—questions that I'm sure every child has.

All of this wondering gave me a sense of fate, a sense of being guided in an ordered universe that I later identified as

coming from some divine power. Fate tosses us together,
breaks us apart, and pushes us on. We do a lot to control it.
But there is always that spark of fate, and somehow the
hand of God, about everything we do. I believe that. It's one
of my earliest convictions.

Later observations bear this attitude out. In this country
most people move around a lot. They move their homes,
their businesses, and their families, sometimes thousands of
miles. It's kind of like the urge to make pilgrimages, like in
the Bible. That movement makes it rather chancy how you
meet, team up, and court people. For some it is a disaster of
almost fatal proportions for the soul.

Fate drew my parents together. My father was born on a
farm. Tobacco was the biggest crop. It was really a well-run,
diversified farm, much more so than most in that area. The
others just raised tobacco and cotton. Dad's family was
large, like most families around there. They were all in the
tradition of the old pioneer families around there. They
settled, raised a large family, worked hard and saw the children move on to new horizons. Some did stay and develop
new endeavors thereabouts. Some hung around to fight over
available farm land and estates. So it went.

Dad and his brothers were a hell-raising bunch. I get the
feeling that everybody around there lived high and hard. I
mean they really lived life to its fullest. Some put down
roots, and really dug in. And they had one rip-roaring time
doing it.

One reason for that is because my father's family had
Indian blood. I'm part Cherokee Indian. So, when anyone
says I look kind of like a wild Indian, well I guess I sure
enough do. But the men are all tall, rangy and athletic. The
Indian side came from Grandmother Perry, a Cherokee. Her
maiden name was Jacobs, a fine old Indian name. I never met
her. Both she and Grandfather Perry died before I was ever
even born. Dad was one of eleven children. And so was my
mother. I don't think I could get into a fight anyplace in

northern Florida or southern Georgia without hitting a relative.

My father and his brothers ran away from home when they were very young. Grandfather Perry was really something else. In some ways he was a very wicked man. He was cruel. The boys didn't like being at home in any way, shape or form. As soon as they could make it away, they ran. They escaped. That gave all of them a close tie, a common bond that drew them closer together than most brothers I've seen.

I've heard one story many times about my Uncle Arthur, my father's next younger brother, trying to run away from home. He went into his daddy's coat and took fifty cents; that was to make his escape with, and to make his way in the world. But his father caught up with him at the train station. He took the buggy whip and whipped him—not for trying to run away from home, but for stealing that fifty cents! He couldn't have cared less about the running away part. But stealing fifty cents, that was too much! He beat him, horsewhipped him, and threw him into the buggy and drove back home. Well, Grandmother Perry tried to help Uncle Arthur take off his shirt, but he had been whipped so hard that she had to take oil and soak the shirt because the whiplash had driven the cloth right into the flesh.

Granddaddy Perry was a pretty rough customer. One time one of my uncles told me of an incident about a horse that Granddaddy owned. The horse wouldn't take the bit, so Granddaddy beat the horse. It hadn't been the first time, but this time the horse managed to wrench free. It broke loose, turned on him, and tried to kick and trample him to death. But Granddaddy got away and ran to the house. The house had a high porch across the front, as many old Southern houses do. The horse chased him and was really closing fast when Granddaddy managed to throw himself under the porch to safety. The horse was so crazed that it ran into the porch and broke its neck.

My father and most of his brothers grew into disciplinarians, too, but they were just. My father, especially, had a great sense of fair play. He genuinely loved people, especially his family. But he'd get after us if he thought we were misbehaving.

Dad was a splendid, powerful father figure to me, and to all of us. He was a large man. I remember him as huge. I guess he must have been about the same size that I am now. I remember his dark swarthy complexion, his piercing yet smiling eyes and his steel gray hair.

My father had charm and authority. He made the decisions, and that was it. That was the law. Of course, he spoiled us in many ways. Anything we wanted, we got. Christmas time at our house was just wild. He was really so proud of his boys. I remember my mother used to say that they had originally wanted either a football team or a baseball team. But after my littlest brother was born, my mother became ill, and it was not possible for her to have any more children. So she used to tell Dad that she was going to settle for a five-piece orchestra. As it turned out, I disliked most sports, and only one son became a really good musician. Mother used to describe all of us as being able to sing, "Not good, but real loud."

The only sport I really loved was swimming. I can't remember the time when I couldn't swim. One of my earliest recollections of swimming was at a place called Blue Sink near Tallahassee. There was a system of lakes there. One of them is said to have had no bottom. It was deep enough that no one had been able to measure it. Well, I was there with my folks and a neighbor lady one time. The grown-ups were really cutting up, and my father picked up this lady that was with us and threw her right into the water. Well, it wasn't until he threw her in that he discovered that she couldn't swim. She got all hysterical. Father jumped into the water to save her, and Mother jumped in to help. I thought it was just a marvelous way that these grown-ups were carrying on. So, as the rescue was being effected, they looked up and saw me walk right into the water and disappear! They rescued me. I'd just stepped into a hole. I was still only a child then; I think I was only three. I cannot remember not being able to swim, even then. No matter how scared they were, I still felt that I must have sort of swum out of that hole on my own steam. I recall that that swimming event was a time when I was just getting to know my father. The first couple or three years of my life he'd been gone. He'd had to serve a prison sentence instigated by the Revenuers.

When I was about four or five, I used to go swimming in Bethel Lake. It used to scare my mother because she would be floating along on her inner tube in this little country pond right out in the middle of nowhere, and I'd paddle up and tag along in the water right around her. It would upset her no end. She'd tell me she was going to whip me if I didn't get back where it was shallower.

My father was the type of man who was convinced that nothing was impossible. He really took his time with all of us. And I think all of us have a lot of that in us today. He was gone sometimes, but he spent the time he saved to be with us really enjoying himself. He'd get us all together and we'd all go out swimming. That was really his sport, too. It was something that he loved. And we all developed a love for it too. There were times when Mother didn't go, and it was just Dad and my brothers and me. He'd bundle us all up, and we'd all take off. We had a real wow of a time. It was that kind of atmosphere around the house that I think of so often when I recall my boyhood.

Of course, nowadays, when I get into my suit to go swimming and take a run down the sand toward the water, I hear people saying, "There goes our pastor. He's still trying to learn to walk on water!" It's a great sport—the swimming, not the walking.

My dad was a sport in other ways, too. Especially before he married. My Uncle Wallace told me that he and my dad used to have some wild times. Dad lived near Uncle Wallace and Aunt Fanny. Both of them were kind of hellions, too. Dad always drove the swankiest and sportiest car on the street. He used to get his car and come over and pick up

Uncle Wallace and they'd go off "jerking," as they called it down there. That meant that they went out to meet the girls and have a night on the town. It always made Aunt Fanny mad. She knew what was up. Dad was still a bachelor. He'd always let Uncle Wallace know about when he'd be by to pick him up. Then, he'd drive into the big circular driveway and honk the horn of his car. Uncle Wallace would charge out of the house, and jump off the porch onto the back of the car. Dad never stopped, just slowed the car enough to catch Uncle Wallace. They'd circle around in front, around that driveway, while Uncle Wallace climbed in, and then they'd tear off. Aunt Fanny got really fed up with that routine. So one time, when she saw this, she was all primed. Uncle Wallace came charging out of the house to make his vaulting leap onto Dad's car. Aunt Fanny hollered, "Where are you going, Wallace?" He didn't answer; he just went through the same routine. But Aunt Fanny had a bullwhip, and she took off after them as fast as she could go. She started popping Uncle Wallace right on the rump with that whip. And Uncle Wallace yelled, "Troy, if you don't fire up this car and get going to outrun Fanny, I'm going to get killed!" Well, Dad didn't go all that fast, and Aunt Fanny just ran as hard as she could down the lane to the street, cracking that whip, popping Uncle Wallace right on the hind end. She was as mad as a hornet that they would go out somewhere like that. But they were that kind of people. After Dad married Mother he settled down a lot, and we never heard anything more of that kind of episode.

My mother's people, her grandparents and parents, settled on the Island Homestead. And that's still in her family. She came from a large family, too. There were eleven children, just like with my father's people.

Mother's brother, Uncle Mark, was the sheriff of the county for a long time. He bought out all of the other members of the family. They were all well paid, and he ended up owning Island Homestead. When he died, his widow, my Aunt Meredith, inherited the property. I think she must own just about half of the whole county. My father's people owned the property next to Island Homestead. And that's still in the Perry family.

My mother was born in Hamilton County, near Jasper, very close to the Georgia line. I guess it's about eighty miles from Tallahassee. She lived on a very diversified farm, what's often called a dirt farm, and she developed a very tolerant and philosophical attitude early in her life. She, and the rest of the family, lived a happy, close, loving life. They were rough, too. They even made all of their own toys. They were a self-reliant tribe. Somehow I think they were fatalistic too. She went to school through the tenth grade. That was as far as school went in that neck of the woods.

Tragedy struck her early in life. When she was only eleven, her father was drowned in a flash flood. There had been some very heavy rains, and he went down to a lower pasture to drive some cattle to higher ground. He was trapped there by the rushing water, and no escape was possible. His death gave Mother her first real experience in making a new life after a shattering tragedy.

Mother had married rather young. But her first marriage didn't work out, and she didn't try to stick with it. She got a divorce. So, when she met my father she was free, and still very young. She had gone to visit an older sister in Tallahassee, and helped out in a store that her sister ran there. A restaurant was connected to the store, so she waited on customers in both places. My father came into the restaurant, and she waited on him. Well, he upset her. Her sister said to her, "What's the matter?" and Mother asked who that flirt was that was eyeing her. Dad was wearing a white panama suit and white shoes. He was a real dude.

Her sister said, "Oh, that's Troy Perry. Just ignore him."

I don't think my mother did. Some spark had flashed between them. He fell in love with her right there, and he swept her off her feet. Some say he chased her 'til she caught him. Maybe so. It was a short, whirlwind romance. And it lasted as long as he lived. They were really the happiest people I can remember.

Mother was loyal and loving. She devoted her life to my father. That's the way she was raised. And that was just the way it was. I remember their energy and stamina. I recall Mother as the traditional Southern woman, the typical mother of the South. She felt her place was in her home, and that was it. She had been raised on a farm, and she felt that it was a wife's duty to react in a certain way, and to do certain things. She was really a homemaker. She was completely loyal to her husband, and to his children. That was the way it was supposed to be.

I think when I got to know Dad, when I was around three years old, he kind of overwhelmed me. We loved each other so much. I wanted to be like him. I think this is why I am kind of like a strong older brother, like a father in some ways to my younger brothers. I had to help them with their thoughts just like I have had to help people around me today in my church work.

Maybe getting to know and love my father later in my life, as a toddler, added to my keen sense of curiosity. I wondered about him. Where did fathers come from? I used to ponder that. Maybe part of my sexual curiosity goes back to that time. Maybe it has affected my fascination with metaphysics and mysticism, my fatalism. I don't know. It gave me a sense of changing scenes, of that kaleidoscope wherein the pattern always changes, and can never be the same again after that first fleeting moment, another image, another momentary experience.

Momentary experiences are largely how I recall essential episodes of my childhood such as school, and some of the people I knew. I recall the strange dry chalk-dust smell of the old red brick schoolhouse I first went to. Right now I can recall the smells of those strange cleaning compounds that seep through all institutions—a smell I recall from schools, army kitchens, and, more recently, jail. They are the smells of gymnasiums and of the whole biology of our presence on this planet.

I went to Sealy Memorial Grammar School. I think it was named to honor some teacher. During my last year there, they added a new wing. It was just marvelous. I couldn't believe it. I'd never seen anything like the lights they had installed. When they were turned on you couldn't see them. Well, that's how I was introduced to indirect lighting. But I just couldn't get over it. The heaters for the rooms had been built right into the floor. It was one of the most modern schools in the county. And it was surely the most up-to-date public building in the city. Everyone was so proud of it. My whole reaction to that school is typical of the sense of awe I had as I was coming up.

In school I either did well or just horribly. I remember I failed the second grade. I didn't really like the first grade either. I don't remember why. It seems to me that I hated the teacher. The teacher was always getting onto me because I was always running around pulling up the little girls' dresses. Believe it or not, that was my main sin, I guess. But it sure upset everybody—no end!

There was one little girl named Wanda. I'll never forget her name. She was the ugliest little girl I ever remember seeing in my whole life. But I used to propose marriage to her, and that really upset her. Well, she went right home and told her mother. Her father was the pastor of a Baptist church there in Tallahassee. We were in the second grade, Wanda and I. Maybe that's why I failed. At any rate, I recall the teacher calling me out of the classroom, and there was Wanda and her mother. I mean I was really outnumbered. Wanda's mother and the teacher both scored me off no end for my proposing marriage to Wanda. But what really got them up tight was my going around the school grounds and pulling up Wanda's dress. Like I said, I've always been curious. But I guess I got over that kind of curiosity in time.

School, the rest of it, just kind of sinks out of sight. I remember that I had the idea of working out a life that strictly followed religious lines. The Southern Pentecostal churches were all pretty rigid, and I followed the doctrine at home and at school—as much as I could. I deviled everyone with it. And, I would actually lead the Sunday school. It made me feel so good. I even preached on the school steps when I was in junior high school. I probably seemed as far out as today's long-bearded, long-haired hippie. I drew a few stares, but no stones.

The rest of school speeds by as though the merry-go-round were tilting. I was fascinated by life's processes. I know I went endlessly to school, made friends, had fights, made enemies, got hurt, got over it, made up with fellows after a fight and tried to overcome and satisfy my impatient curiosity about how things worked, and why. I still carry a lot of that with me today. I remember the heat of summer, the hot, sticky, relentless, exhausting heat that seared every fiber of everything and never ended. I recall how that heat gave way to cold, the strange, wet, frosty, whitish cold of northern Tallahassee winters. The cold had a kind of physical presence that was almost like fog, the kind of fog that engulfs you as though you've been sucked up whole into a mouth, a gigantic yawning cavern. In winter the trees suddenly swim out of the mist like ghostly spires. My throat would go dry then. And my saliva would run cold. Frost hung in the air, and it was hard to breathe. But I remember whiteness and stickiness, and either cold or warmth. Warmth was reassuring.

During my eleventh year, I spent some time on my uncle's country farm. On one occasion I had to share a bed with one of the neighbor boys. He was older than I.

We were both restless, and we tried to sleep. I relaxed, thinking that sleep would surely come. When he thought I was asleep, he pushed back the sheets exposing his whole body. I watched through half-closed eyes in the dim silvery grayness of the still night. He clutched his penis in his hand and rubbed, caressed, and pulled on it. He just couldn't stop. As his movements became jerkier, his whole body writhed.

His breathing became deeper and kind of forced. I stared, not daring to move or speak. What was I really watching here? I felt vague stirrings within me, yet I froze in the warm stillness, spellbound. After a few minutes that seemed like ages, he gasped, gritted his teeth, snorted, moaned and let go. Deep sighs escaped him.

My joy was too much for me to contain. He had not been in pain, yet he had seemed close to it. I realized that what I had actually seen was something that had to do with life and the creative forces. I was sure then that I was seeing in his semen some form of what I had been, and what we all have been. It is one of the first living forms. It is the drop of magical fluid that brings us to life and follows us to the grave. It is older than man himself. It changes and develops into other forms. In these magical drops all of life is contained in miniature. That is surely one of God's greatest miracles. I knew that as I watched this miracle for the first time. I exulted.

My hands would not remain still. They were drawn like metal to a lodestar, to that attribute of my former self, that dying sperm. I touched this wonderous substance, but when I did, a look of shock crossed the young man's face. He was frightened, and moved away. How could I convey my feelings to him? I thought of his smile, and watched him take the sheet and begin to wipe away with two or three swift strokes the remnants of his ecstasy. He looked calm, and knowing. I asked him to stop wiping. But he didn't. I asked what had happened. He tried to explain it to me. He didn't do it often, just when he got nervous or excited. And, yes, it was such fun. He explained about babies, and what our parents did. Of course, I knew that already. I had already tried, in my own way, and had had my own first experiments and experiences. I was sure that I was getting primed for some kind of thrilling sexual happenings.

Northern Florida is a land of tall pines and dense woods. Those stands of white pine filled me with awe. They always had a sense of mystery about them. They were both inviting and forbidding, as if warning me away.

Two weeks before Christmas the weather was alternately cold and warm. It got warm and nice out in the afternoons, and then turned really cold at night. I remember that we still didn't have a Christmas tree up in our home. My parents promised me that I could go out with a friend of mine, a neighbor boy, and cut a tree. We would go to the Bird's Woods and bring back the trees, holly, and misteltoe for both families. My friend, Daniel, was nearly seventeen. He attended a Seventh Day Adventist parochial school in southern Georgia, and he was home for Christmas vacation. He belonged to that church, I remember. But I recall that he was not really a good member. He ate bacon. And my mother told me that if he really was a good church member of that religion, he shouldn't.

Daniel was tall, much taller than I. He was really about six feet, I guess. He lived with his mother and family about eight blocks from our house. His father was dead. He had two older brothers, one in the army, the other working in Virginia.

Daniel had coal black hair that laid in thick locks over his forehead, like a cascade. His teeth reminded me of the Biblical stories about "sheep that came up from the washing after having been even shorn, each bearing a twin, and none barren among them." His smile was so winning. Daniel was a Biblical beauty. His lips were kind of a dark red. I remember them as a blur of scarlet. He walked so surely and proudly.

When Daniel got to our house, he talked to my father and mother for what seemed hours. I thought we'd never get started. I was surprised to hear my mother tell him not to rush off, that he'd only been there ten minutes. But finally, we did get away.

We walked down Sixth Avenue. It had just recently been paved. We went towards Bovard Avenue, and talked about everything. Then Daniel became quiet. Two girls passed us, walking on the other side of the street. Daniel looked over at the two of them. He smiled and licked his lips, clucked and said he'd really like to take both of them to bed and do it—do something—to them. I blushed. I was scared someone might hear him use that word. My parents said that it was a dirty word. But he saw me look down. He reached over and gave me a little punch on the shoulder and said, "Aw, come on, you'd like to hump 'em, too." I could just have fallen right through the sidewalk.

Bird's Woods. Strange. Inside Bird's Woods it was warm, but it looked cold. The sun was shining, but the trees were dark. Small bushes grew everywhere, and thrusting out from among them were pine trees. The ground was carpeted with a pine straw that was slick and crunchy underfoot.

We hunted for just the right tree for over an hour. We got some holly. Later, we found mistletoe. We had made a little headquarters in a quiet, warm clearing in the woods. There we put our coats, the holly, the mistletoe, and went off in search of trees. I think we must have talked incessantly. We hadn't seen each other for months. Finally, Daniel spied two trees that were just right. They were like twins. We chopped them down in no time, and carted them back to our place in the clearing. Well, we had really run around a lot, and worked up a sweat. Now we had to be careful not to get cold.

Daniel asked me if I was cold. I sat down to rest, and nodded my head yes. He put his arms around my shoulders and hugged me to him. My hands were cold. I put them in his lap, between his legs, to warm them. I smiled at him. And Daniel looked strangely at me, but he smiled back. His grin lingered. And then, as he held me, I felt his strength enfold me. His lips brushed the skin of my cheeks. They nibbled at the flesh of my face. I held very still. I was cold, but I tingled all over, and felt warm inside. Daniel's hands moved to my lap. He fumbled with the buttons on my pants and looked and undid them one at a time. He smiled. I felt the swelling in his groin where I hid my hands. Then finally his hands, cold, and yet warm, took out my own organ. I hesitated, but his head ducked quickly down, and his mouth replaced his hands. The warmth of that moment, the surging, the feeling that I could not resist, that I must yield up, swept over me. I leaned back against the oak's great trunk. I thought, Oh God, Oh God . . . Oh God. . . .

Later on as we grew older we had other times together. We began to branch out a little. There were other kids my own age, and we all experimented as much as we could.

For me, those episodes were a kind of secret that was all part of coming up. Nothing was ever said. But we did have other kinds of hidden knowledge in our family. And nothing was ever said about them either. For instance, the fact that my father was a bootlegger was something that was just never mentioned. Yet, he was actually the biggest bootlegger in northern Florida. In addition, he was also a very successful businessman. He had a thriving farm, a contracting and construction business, and a small chain of filling stations. He was a wheeler-dealer. He was always on the move.

Mother did a lot of work with my father. She handled much of the administration of his legitimate businesses for him. He couldn't read or write. He wouldn't know his name if it was in block letters on a billboard across the street. My mother taught him how to write his signature. She read everything to him, and she took care of all his correspondence. But my father was a mathematical wizard. He could really work out all the math problems in his head, and just astound everyone. When it came to money, he was really a shrewd businessman, and a good one. We all knew what else he did. But it was a very quiet thing. It was an awareness that came, a kind of feeling, not consciously realizing, yet knowing. It was a hidden knowledge. Almost like the love that dares not speak its name. My mother looked up to my father so much. He was twenty years older, and he represented such a strong influence in her life. They relied upon each other totally. There were many funny things that happened. I'm sure that all my relatives could tell one incident about Dad and his bootlegging, and really have you rolling on the floor. But it was the same bootlegging that brought about my father's sudden death in a flaming horror that still pains us all.

But this is one of my mother's favorite stories about Dad's other business. Mother and my Aunt Mary were in Mother's house. The law just walked right in on them while they were at the kitchen sink doing the dishes. My mother was startled. She asked what they were doing there, and they said, "All right, where's it hid?"

She said, "I don't know what you're talking about!" They tramped through the house and looked around. They did have a search warrant. But they didn't find anything. And they left. Just as they left, my father pulled up behind them and got out; they had a few words to say back and forth, but the police hadn't found anything. Dad ordered them off the place, and they left. Dad turned and walked into the house just as a five gallon jug burst in the attic and whisky started seeping through the ceiling. The moonshine flowed down that night.

There had been other close calls, and some a little too close. I know that when I was just a tiny baby my father went to prison. He was there during the first two years of my life. I met him, really for the first time, when he got out. I was almost three.

But once out, he really made up for lost time. When he got squared away, and back in business, there was just no stopping my father. He supplied the bootleg booze to all the politicians there in Tallahassee. That was what finally brought about his doom. I was only twelve years old when my father was killed. It happened in June 1952. I remember going to bed, and waking up to Mom's screaming. It was all so unreal and so weird. People came to our house and broke the news to my mother. The law never did come to tell us that he was killed.

This is pretty much how it happened. I had a cousin, Clay, who was eighteen and a real hellion. He was my aunt's son. He was a super-heterosexual, and was kind of like James

Dean—a real rebel, but with a motorcycle. He ran against the law. By that, I mean he taunted the police and needled them. And they started rousting him, too. Quietly and inevitably, the situation was building to a clash. They watched him, followed him, stopped him, searched him and made life as tough for him as they could. And he really egged them on, and then defied them, just laid them out, every chance he got.

One time he was chased through Tallahassee on his motorcycle. They couldn't catch him, so they shot the tires on his motorcycle. He spun out. Well, I know that my father helped him out of that scrape. My father liked Clay a lot. In many ways they were cut from the same piece of goods: dashing romantic rebels doomed for a tragic finish.

My father was able to help Clay because it was rumored that my father not only paid off the police, but he also supplied the governor with liquor. Leon County was a dry county in the state of Florida. No liquor could be sold there, so it was really fertile field for bootleggers, and for boozehounds.

Clay was always under surveillance of one kind or another, and the lawmen watched my father pretty carefully, too. Every once in a while my father would lie low, or take a business trip for a time. These were short periods, though. And then after the campaign to clean up that county and to drive the rascals out would die down, he'd be riding high again. Well, the early morning that the killing took place, my father went downtown with Clay. There was a gas war on, so they went to one of Father's service stations and picked up some gasoline in large, five-gallon jugs. They put them in the car and started off to another filling station. My father was driving his brand new Lincoln; he loved big cars. The police spotted him with Clay, and just started to give chase. Rather than stop and let them see what was in the jugs, my father took off. He outran them, but I guess he couldn't stand the success of his escape. I think there just had to be more drama than that for both my father and Clay.

Anyway, he made a U-turn and drove back near the police. Well, flaunting their victory that way just was more than the law could stand. They couldn't tolerate seeing this big, shiny Lincoln that they hadn't caught getting away again. So they took out after it.

Witnesses said they heard gunshots, the screech of tires, and the rending crash of the car turning over. Then somehow the jugs of gasoline all exploded. They were both incinerated, my father and Clay, in a horrible fire. They couldn't be rescued. People said they heard them scream. We were told that when the police got to the scene, my father shouted to them, begged them to shoot him, to kill him, and to end his awful pain and misery. It was brief and violent, the fiery way his life ended so suddenly. It plunged our world at home into black despair. We didn't realize it then, but our world was gone, completely shattered. I recall that was a hot June night in 1952. The smell of insect repellent hung in the early morning air, giving it a rather sweetish and sickly fragrance. I lay in my bed, totally nude, thinking about my thirteenth birthday, which would be the end of the following month. It was impossible to sleep. I thought of my four brothers, my mother and father, the neighbors, the people down the street, school, something to eat, a drink of water and my prayers. I said my prayers again. And finally my eyes must have closed.

I heard a wailing scream, and I jumped out of bed. It was already morning. The scream sounded again and again, and I knew that it was my mother. I ran to her. I rushed also to my brothers. They were awakening. I couldn't believe the reason she was crying as she swept us up in her arms. Our daddy was dead. Our daddy was dead! But that couldn't be. I pulled away. I wept in rage and disbelief. Mother tried to comfort me and her other sons.

We became ghostlike figures walking through the house as people hurried in and conversed in hushed tones, and left. Morning faded into late afternoon. I was desperate. I ran out of the house and down the street to Daniel's. He wasn't

there, but his mother urged me to come in. She hugged me
to her as I tried to push past. Oh, I wished to God that I could
have told her how I felt. But I could not. I sat waiting for
Daniel. The phone rang and it was he calling. His mother
told him that I was there. As she talked she kept looking at
me, nodding her head and smiling as though she understood.
How could anyone? She hung up and said that we would go
and pick up Dan at his sister's house on the outskirts of
Tallahassee.

Old Bainbridge Road winds out of Tallahassee as sinu-
ously as the Willicuchi River glided past our farm in Hamilton County. Daniel's mother drove us along this series of
curves, the same course upon which my father had raced to
his death. We slowed down and stopped as we approached
the crash site because people had gathered around the
wreck. For some reason the burned-out body of the car was
still there with guard rails around it. It was dangerous. People stopped and milled around recounting stories of the
disaster.

Before Mrs. Perkins could stop me, I jumped out of the car
and ran forward. Here was the spot where my father had fled
from the arms of the law into the arms of death. Some said
that they heard the wail of police sirens, then the pistol
shots, then the screech of tires, and then the crash of the
automobile, and then the explosion. One man said he heard
my father beg the police to shoot him. Then the fire con-
sumed him and the car, and burned everything. Finally his
screams ended as death embraced him.

I pushed my way through the crowd, and stopped behind
a man who stooped down and picked something up from the
wreck. It was a black piece of my father's hair and scalp. The
man stooped down again. I screamed. I felt sick. I ran. And
I cursed as I ran, cursed and screamed and shouted. It was
my first time on the killing ground.

I didn't know it then, but I was running and shouting and
crying my way into a new beginning of life. I was running
into manhood much faster than I was prepared to accept. I

was older than any of my brothers, a good three years older. They needed me. My mother needed me. She was so lost. I tried to help her. But I had such a sense of loss myself, and a sense of failure.

Of course, I turned to God. But I could not find an adequate answer. I looked to Christ. But he seemed to me to be only the Angel of Death. Perhaps he was the Angel of Death in disguise. I recalled his picture, and how he appeared in all of the plaster art work dealing with the crucifixion: his hair long, his eyes either dark brown or blue, his looks ethereal. He seemed to be more than a comely lad. I think I felt that He was a seductive Angel. I had loved Him. But He had taken my father. Why had He not taken me? That was a question I would ponder for the rest of my adolescence, and until I was made ready to begin my own true mission.

Meanwhile everyone tried to help Mother. She was so lost. So hurt. Mother hired a private detective to find out if the law was at fault. There was no coroner's jury held; in the south we do things just a little differently. Father's death made the front pages of every newspaper in Florida. It was conceded by some that the law was at fault, but the police would not admit it. People kept coming around and saying that the law had done a wrong thing. But what can you do? That's just the way it was. I'll never forget the funeral. It was really large, probably larger than it would normally have been, because my father's death had been so melodramatic. The mortician opened his funeral home to Negroes for the first time. It was unheard of for a black person to enter that funeral home. But my father owned a lot of houses over in French town—that was the Negro quarters in Tallahassee. A lot of those people worked for my father. We had maids that worked for us, and like most middle- and upper middle-class Southerners, we considered them part of the family. One of the maids who worked for us called up and told my mother, "Mrs. Perry, I'm gonna tear that door down if they don't open it and let us go in and say goodbye to Mr. Troy." So Mother called Mr. Calley and asked him to please open the funeral home to the Negroes. Well, he didn't want to, but she insisted. So they did open it—during the hours of six to nine in the evening, I believe. The funeral at the church was an all-white affair, but at the graveyard the Negroes were all standing up on the hillside, waiting. Once everybody had gathered around the coffin, they came down and stood with us too.

My mother was at such a loss. My father's death didn't draw us any closer together because it couldn't. We were already close together, and we all felt the loss so much. It seemed so unreal, that he was actually gone.

But he was. And I began a search that was to take up much of my life, a search that would end only when I had begun my true mission in life. The search began with my father's death. I never understood why he seemed to have chosen that time and place to die. He had courted the Angel of Death, and had been entrapped by it. I was not prepared for the man's role that was thrust upon me. My mother helped. She helped all of us. I felt that I could never do enough to help her. I couldn't get over the loss of my father. I knew that I had been betrayed. His death had done that to me. Yet, I had to go ahead, somehow. But it was my mother who had the most agonizing path ahead of her. In my own frustration and terror, I was to be of little real help to her for some time. I had to flee for survival leaving her to gather her own strengths, and push on as best she could.

Chapter Two
Coming Up

Mother had always had someone to take care of her, to watch out for her and to handle all the business affairs. This was true of her entire adult life, I'm sure. My father had done that. It was his role. But here she was now, a widow with five children. Dad had left Mother with plenty of money. She didn't have to worry about anything. But after he was killed, something just went out of her. I'm sure she felt as I did, as we all did. We had to get away from that killing ground. Mother just couldn't cope with the part of his business she had dealt with. She was numb. And she was a setup. Well, sure enough, some fellow happened along, and realized it. He kind of took over. He set out to woo and win her. He did. She relied heavily upon him. Six months after my father was killed, she remarried.

The new man of the house was so unlike my father in so many ways. I just couldn't get used to him. He'd get drunk, and I'd never seen my father take a drink. He may have gotten drunk at some time, but I never knew about it. This fellow used foul language, and we'd never heard that kind of language around the house, never in front of my mother, and never from my father. When the new man got drunk, he wasn't above picking up whatever was handy—usually a rubber hose—and giving one of us a whipping. Usually I was the one. I'd rather it was me than my brothers. I felt so helpless. It was all so different somehow. I was really going through one hell of a time in my life. This man was not a businessman. He squandered everything. He resented all of us. But I think he thought I was the biggest threat of all, probably because I tried to stand between him and my little brothers.

To make it worse, we had moved. We were alone, friendless and strangers. Mother had sold out lock, stock and barrel and moved to Daytona Beach, Florida. There my mother and her new husband bought a restaurant and a motel, a deep-sea fishing boat and a large fishing camp. It was pretty, quite a spread. But I hated school, even though I loved that whole area. This fellow was good to my mother, but I felt so out of place that I decided that the only thing I could do was to run away.

I planned my strategy carefully. I never knew until years later that I was really forcing the issue of our home life, forcing my mother to choose between her new husband and her sons. It was a cruel pressure. It was a relentless push. My mother emerged from it with an incredible strength and courage, the kind that pioneer women made famous in this country. My mother showed that she was of that same stock.

I had written to my aunt, who lived out in El Paso, Texas, and I asked her to write me at the local high school that I attended. It seems so strange and somehow funny to me now. The plot was so complex, and so transparent. But she was as serious as I was. She wrote me at the school and said, "Go to your uncle's in Georgia, first, and I'll get you out of there." Well, that I knew I could do. But I was afraid. It would still have to be a touch and go affair. So the morning I was going to leave, I got up a little earlier. I had hardly been able to sleep the night before. I polished my shoes, and put on clean clothes. I had a shirt, clean pants and a warm coat. I'd saved my money, but I went downstairs and took money out of the cash register—just so I would have enough money to leave on. Then I rode the school bus and got off in front of the school. I had taken only my tooth brush and tooth paste with me; that's all I could get in my coat pocket. I felt strange all over. I got off the bus, then walked from the school across the bridge to the Greyhound bus station. I was scared to death. I knew that the new husband was supposed to go uptown that morning. And oh, if he caught me up there, that would just be it! I had timed it so that I would arrive at the Greyhound station just five minutes before the bus left. Well, somehow it didn't really all go according to plan. I got there fifteen minutes before the bus left, so I went and purchased my ticket, and then I locked myself in a pay booth in the men's restroom. I sat there just scared to death. Finally, I heard the bus being announced over the loud-speaker. I went right out and got on the bus.

All the way to the Georgia line it was just about heart-attack time. I kept looking back out of the window; I was so worried. I worried about Mom and my brothers, too, but I knew that if I didn't leave I'd surely die. I recall that just before I'd left, I'd wished that her new husband was dead. He was beating me almost daily, and I made up my mind one day that I'd kill him. I had that on my mind for quite a spell. I remember once I went into the house and into his bedroom, and I took his pistol out of his drawer. I couldn't find any bullets. I decided then that even death didn't want that evil man, so he was spared for a time at least.

Since I couldn't figure out some way of killing him, I knew that I had to escape. That would change everything. What had prompted me to go at that time was that my stepfather's younger brother had moved in with us. He brought a young friend with him who was a sailor in the merchant marines. He was only going to stay for a couple of weeks, but during the time that I was able to stand it, he really had everything stirred up. The young sailor came and got into bed with me toward the end of that last week; I remember waking slightly as he did. Then, just after he slid under the covers, I felt him roll onto my body. He was trying to enter me in some way. I was scared, and I started to scream. He covered my face with a pillow, and pushed my head down so no one could hear. I fought and squirmed, and got away from him. And I made up my mind right then and there that I would run away. I had to escape somehow.

Things sure had changed. Every summer, since I was about eight years old, my father had sent us to visit his brother up in Tipton, Georgia. It was only eighty miles from Tallahassee. And now, less than a year after my father's death here, I was an exile from my own home, a runaway looking for any out. But once over the Georgia state line, I just breathed a big sigh of relief. I knew they couldn't take me back now without really causing problems. I knew my aunt and uncle would help me.

As I rode along I knew that my heart would just break if things didn't work out. I'd just die. But I prayed. Not a lot. I couldn't. I was too upset. People get that way. But I was sure that things would really work out. I finally got off the bus, and had to hitchhike in the dark, in the blackest night I can remember. I walked part of the way. The house was out in the country, and I thought I'd never get there. I finally came to a dirt road that went back in through the woods up to their farm, and to their neighbors' farms, and I just started walking. Some kid came along in a truck, and took me to a fork in the road. He pointed the way, and I set out. A dog in the next house started barking. That sound of the yelping barks followed me clear down the road. I finally got there. I went up to this dark door, and I knocked. Right away I heard one of my cousins say, "Come in." Well, I did. And he nearly dropped dead. I've never seen anyone so scared.

It was like he was seeing a ghost or something. It seems that just a few minutes before I got there they'd heard the wind rattling the door. He was sure that it was someone, so he got everybody up. Well, his daddy made him open the door. And there was no one there. So everybody started back to bed. Then I knocked. And his daddy made him go to the door again. I must have been rather timid with my knocking because they still thought it was just the wind. Well, when I stepped in through that door into the dim light, I think they all turned several shades paler. They just stared a minute. My aunt was the first one to snap to. So she bustled around, and hustled up something for me to eat. I told them why I'd run away. I told them that mother's new husband drank a lot and that he beat me. I was so relieved just spilling the whole story. I laughed. I cried. And I was sure hungry. My aunt put her arms around me and just said, "Well, you did the right thing, I guess. You better hurry and get to bed. You'll have to go to school in the morning." And I did. I only missed one day of school: the day I was traveling on that bus.

The next day the sheriff came and asked if she had a visitor. And she said, "Yeah." She knew him by his first name. Most families, the old families there, did.

So he said, "Could I talk to him?"

She said, "No."

"Why not?" the sheriff asked.

"Well, he's in school."

He must have smiled at her, and she told me she smiled at the sheriff, and he said, "Well! So you've already got him in school, have you?"

And she said, "Yeah."

And he said, "Well, I'll write—or wire—the Florida authorities about it. He's all right, I reckon." And they let me go on my own.

I suppose I should pause to say, meanwhile back in Florida. . . . I had really worried about what would happen to my brothers and to my mother. I knew my running away would make a stir. But it made a lot more waves than I figured it would.

That day, when I didn't come home, and when they found out that I hadn't been to school, my mother almost went crazy. She told her husband, "If you've done something to Troy, so help me God, I'll kill you!" And she meant it, too. She had visions of me floating down the Halifax River that ran right through the property there. She thought he really might have hit me on the head or something, and that I'd got drowned before I surfaced. I guess you could say that my mother is a really formidable woman. She must have had a lot of anger and tension that she'd been storing up. And I think she must have let it all go that night, when I didn't show. I knew that it would hurt my mother, but I felt I had to run to survive. It was just that simple.

So, when she got the telegram that I was all right, she made up her mind to act. Her husband went on out in the morning to take a group out deep sea fishing. And, as soon as he was out of her sight, my mother packed her children and whatever she could take that she really needed into her new Mercury, and cleared out. She got the car out of the insurance after my father was killed. My mother was determined to educate her boys. So she took books and encyclopedias, their clothes, and what she would really need. She left behind her silverware, and furniture, and a lot of her keepsakes. She was free. That was important. She shed everything that wasn't part of her. And she lost all that she left behind, including the property. She made no more payments, and neither did he. They both lost material things. But she was so relieved because she had made her decision. She was really and truly free. She was scared and she was alone with four small boys, and one on the loose. She was striking out, maybe making her first blow for Women's Lib. She never looked back. She moved to a motel in Winter Haven, Florida. She set herself up there with the boys, put them in school, and set about to make it all work out.

Mother wrote me and told me how my hasty departure

had affected them. She forgave me for leaving as I did and begged me to write. Up in Georgia my life had sharply changed. I loved school. I got along with everybody. Mother wrote to say that if I really was bent on staying there I could if I thought it would help me to find myself. But she said I mustn't stay too long, and I should work hard and do my share. She said she prayed for me, and she would send for me when she needed me, and then I was to come. I agreed.

One thing is for sure. All that I had been through drew me closer to God. I had been preaching. I loved it. I felt it. But I wasn't sure about it being my calling. Not then. Not until I was really dug in up there in Georgia. My uncle always took the whole family to church and to prayer meetings. That was perfectly natural for me. I just kind of grew up in it.

At the first prayer meeting and service that I went to up in Tipton, I heard one of my favorite people preach. She was my Aunt Bea, one of the most influential people in my whole life. She wasn't really an aunt, kind of what you'd call a shirt-tail relative. Aunt Fanny, of the bullwhip fame, had a brother named Robert. And he had married Auntie Bea. I always called him Uncle Bob, and felt close to him too. He was quiet and very warm. Everyone around there was.

Aunt Bea was unlike anyone I ever met anywhere. She was certainly different from anyone I have ever met in my religion. She was the model of a zealot. She had been saved! And I mean she was really saved! But with a vengeance. She had been that traditional lady of pleasure that every small town in the South has. Yes, she was the town whore. She told it all, just like it was, once she'd been saved. Everybody in town knew that she was "the real round-heeled broad, the easiest lay in town." All the men in Lennox knew that. And so did all of their wives, daughters and everyone else —except her husband. He just looked the other way. He never heard anything that was said about her.

Aunt Bea was a very intense person. A lot of our relatives didn't like her, but they put up with her. There wasn't any way not to. Well, she had a Pentecostal conversion, and that is really something else. If you've never seen one, you've missed a real experience—the kind where you have to hang onto to your seat.

In was in the fall of 1939. A new face appeared in the southern part of Georgia. He was the Reverend Rowan, a Holiness preacher. The Holiness church is another name for the Pentecostal church, which some call the Holy Rollers. The people in attendance are moved. The spirit of the Lord seizes them, and they are often literally carried away. The Reverend Rowan was an inspiring force. People came forth and testified. They wept. They moaned. They prayed aloud in a full-voiced frenzy. They sang hymns. They hollered out "amen," and "that's right," and other expressions of agreement during the church services. It was a real old-fashioned Southern Bible Belt revival.

Reverend Rowan was a man of great force and energy, and he was most persuasive. He had been called out of the cotton fields to carry His word to a "dying world." Lennox was the first small town to which God directed him. Reverend Rowan was sure that God would touch the hearts of those sinners who came to hear him. And their hearts were touched. During the first five weeks of his preaching, all went well.

Then, one Sunday afternoon, Aunt Bea wandered into the church where the services were being held. She listened to the message of hope being preached by God's messenger. She became fascinated. And she accepted the words of this man who said that God was all powerful. Bea went forward to the altar and prayed and pleaded. As she was seized with the Holy Ghost, she began to speak and plead in other tongues as the spirit gave her direction. Her whole body shook as she received this anointment.

Well, after that she was a changed woman. She swore that God had directed her to start a fast. She was to eat nothing. She could drink only water. God did not tell her how long to continue this fast, only that she should do it. And she continued her religious zeal.

Her husband, Uncle Bob, watched Bea's fast begin to take effect. It worried him. He didn't mind the religion part of it because now Bea was changed, and even showered him with affection, and she was home every night. But after two weeks of fasting Bea shifted in her form of devotion. She started going to the woods around Lennox and praying. She began to ignore Uncle Bob and everyone else. She seemed somewhat dazed. But she kept up her fast, her wanderings, and her prayers. When anyone asked her why she was doing what she was doing, she would repeat over and over as if by rote, "It's the will of the Father."

Uncle Bob was finally persuaded that Bea had become incompetent. Twenty-two days after she began her fast, he signed the papers to commit her to the state hospital at Millageville. All of Uncle Bob's friends assured him that he had done the right thing. And Bea didn't object. She only smiled at Bob when the sheriff came to pick her up and take her to the hospital up in central Georgia. The sheriff said that she had prayed and spoken in tongues all the way. "That ride wasn't *too* bad," he said.

When Bea was admitted, she kept speaking in tongues. Everyone was very nice to her, but she did irritate them a bit by always replying in an unintelligible tongue. She swore that she spoke only to God. After a week of this type of observation, it was decided that the best thing for her would be heat therapy.

Heat therapy meant being stripped absolutely naked, and placed in a small cell. Hot air was forced into it. The heat on the floor was blistering. Bea urinated on the floor and stood in it to avoid burns. And she spoke in English. She was released and went about the hospital. She came upon one poor woman who kept compulsively tying her hair into knots and pulling them out. Bea saw this, and stopped and rebuked the devil in the name of Jesus. She asked the Lord to heal Sister Mary Jane, as the woman was called. And

Sister Mary Jane was made whole. So were many others. Bea was a healer, and she went about the hospital praying with the other inmates, asking God to heal and save them as He had her. She was released from the hospital after a very short time.

At home, Uncle Bob's quandary was even worse. He missed Bea, whom he really loved, and he took small comfort from those who had commended him upon committing her, for they now ignored him. He also got a great deal of static from the church Bea had joined. The congregation was vocal and very loud about it; the Reverend Rowan decried Uncle Bob's persecution of a God-fearing and religious woman like Aunt Bea. She was a martyr to them. So, half the county was attending those services and giving Bob some pretty weird looks every time he showed up in town. The other half didn't do anything.

After a month of this Bob was pretty lonely. He wanted Bea. Most people had stopped speaking to him. He felt like a leper when he approached people. The only thing he didn't do was go around crying "unclean."

As he tried to figure out what to do, a car pulled up in front of his, and out stepped the Reverend Rowan. He told Uncle Bob that God had instructed him to come over and talk to Bob about his soul and about eternal salvation. Well, that cracked Uncle Bob up. Someone was talking to him, and he started to cry. Reverend Rowan prayed with Uncle Bob, and Uncle Bob became a convert. A week later Aunt Bea was home.

One Sunday afternoon as Reverend Rowan preached, he heard the voice of God speaking to him. He explained this to his more than four hundred faithful crammed into a hot tent. He told them that God was directing him to move on, because his work in Lennox was now completed. But, before he left he wanted to be sure that the town would have its own church building. So he asked someone to give land. One farmer leapt up immediately and offered the church a ten-acre tract just outside of Lennox on the Nashville River.

Reverend Rowan thanked the man, and explained to everyone that that was the way God worked his will. And then he asked for pledges of cash after the harvest so that they could build their church. Over twelve thousand dollars was pledged. That's what you call the Lord's moving, and anointing, and blessing real, real good.

Reverend Rowan explained that God had lead him to Lennox, and how, at first, no one had seemed at all interested in their souls. But God had made a way, and given him the whole county for his harvest. He traced the history of persecution, and the struggle that the church would always have adhering to God's holy ways. In spite of persecution, he stated, God would come upon the scene and bring deliverance. The miracle of Sister Bea is one such example.

Then he said that God had spoken to him that very day about Sister Bea. Everyone turned to Bea. She smiled vaguely. They all knew that he would do more than praise her, and he did. His voice softened almost to a whisper. It was a tense moment. Everyone leaned forward in his chair, trying to catch every word. And he announced that Sister Bea would be the pastor of the Nashville River Holiness Church to be founded there in Lennox.

The congregation went wild. God had spoken to his people. There were shouts of joy and speaking in tongues as that place had never experienced.

Sister Bea was a model for the congregation. She never wore makeup, she never cut her hair, and she wore long sleeved dresses. She was sedate. She was odd, but she was widely respected. She never cared what anyone thought or said. She told everyone just to be himself. "Just be you. Be yourself. Be what you want to be and let others say, think or do what they want," she always advised me. So she must have had a tremendous influence on my early religious searchings. It is an influence that stays with me now.

Bea not only became a pillar of the Lennox church, she became the church. Everyone wanted to hear her speak. She inspired everyone who came into any kind of contact with her. She always got things done through just the weight of her power. She had her own radio show, and went on the air one day a week, giving a one-hour sermon. She didn't organize well. She didn't know how. People came to her either through conversion or curiosity. But she seemed to mesmerize them all.

It was a very unsettling Sunday about two years after Bea had become the pastor of the Nashville River Church. She preached one Sunday that God spoke to her about serpents. She cited the Book of Mark, chapter 16, verses 15-20:

> And these signs shall follow them that believe. In My name they shall lay hands on the sick and they shall recover. They shall speak with new tongues; they shall cast out devils. They shall take up serpents; and if they drink any deadly thing it shall not hurt them.

Bea insisted that it was God's will that they should handle snakes in the church services. She insisted that that would prove to the world that they had a real faith in their God. She read that passage and preached about it. "They *shall* take up serpents," Bea preached. She insisted that the word was *shall* not *maybe* and not *perhaps*.

She explained that this part of the scriptures was as much a part of the Holy Word as John, chapter 3, verse 16:

> For God so loved the world, that He gave His only begotten Son, that whosoever believeth in Him should not perish, but have everlasting life.

Then Bea said that if anyone ever caught and brought a live poisonous snake to the church, she would demonstrate her faith in *her* God.

The following Sunday one of the country farmers, who was not a member of the church, showed up at Bea's regular Sunday service with a sly grin and a large rattlesnake. Everyone in the church was shocked—everyone except Aunt Bea.

She began praying for power, power to overcome Satan in this reptile form. Her body shook with the Holy Ghost's power. She walked to the large fruit jar which held the snake. She reached in and seized the loosely coiled serpent. It did not try to strike her. Sometimes I think she must have let that snake know that it wouldn't dare. But the Lord did move those people. He really was there. She held the snake high over her head. She prayed, and she spoke in tongues.

The congregation went wild. Another woman from her congregation leapt up and started shouting. She felt the power. She came from the same area, and she walked right up to Bea. She took the large snake from Bea and held it high. Like Bea, she felt no ill effects. Then she gave the snake back to Bea, who put it back in the large jar. Bea smiled. She had proved her faith as had others.

Aunt Bea's faith was an endless fountain of energy. God could move! That was her attitude. Period. And that was it. She would go forever. She would do things that helped people. She would go down to Adelle, a little town nearby, and hold street service and take up collections. She was the only woman with her own radio program. It was a compelling religious program.

Thinking about Aunt Bea gives me a sense of images as though I were staring into a kaleidoscope, and turning it, changing the images that appear to be caught in the tube for a brief moment. I recall her zest for life. I think that she reached out and caught her brass ring from her own carrousel. It gave her an insight that is difficult to understand, hard to explain. She was the first to say that I would preach. She really knew it would happen.

When we went to church near Lennox, Georgia, we all wore our Sunday best, and went together. The family I lived with wasn't really big by the standards thereabouts: two girls and two boys, and me along with my aunt and uncle.

The time Aunt Bea prophesied that I'd really be a preacher, we'd had some trouble getting down to church. The service was already underway. We took seats near the front of the building. The congregation was in the midst of a deep, long, and very reverent prayer. Then we were asked to stand and sing. The hymn was "Keep On The Firing Line." I'll never forget it.

Everyone stood as the old, out-of-tune piano sounded the chords. We sang at full voice, and we stamped and shouted and clapped.

> If you're in the battle for the Lord and right,
> Keep on the firing line.
> If you win the battle, brother, you must fight,
> So keep on the firing line.
> Life is but to labor for the Master dear.
> Do not worry, just have faith and good cheer,
> And keep on the firing line.

> Oh you must fight, be brave against all evil,
> Never run nor even lag behind.
> For if you would fight for God and the right,
> Just keep on the firing line.

By the time we got to the chorus, which everyone knew by heart, the whole building was shaking from the forceful hand clapping. As the song went on, I stared at a large framed print hanging behind the altar. It was a picture of the God, Jesus, that we came to worship and sing about and shout his praise. I envied that Galilean who lived almost two thousand years ago. He slept three days in the arms of the Angel of Death, and then returned rejecting him. I hated him for that, for ever knowing death so intimately. The more I looked at that picture, the more I became intrigued with the man called Jesus. I had heard so much about God—my Aunt Bea told of Him—His birth, life, death and resurrection.

The picture showed Him with long, light brown hair hanging to His shoulders, His eyes a deep shade of blue. They stared blankly back at me. His nose was sharp and his chin pointed. The way he wore his hair was not so much

hippie as feminine. As I studied the portrait, I overwhelm-
ingly liked this Israelite. I felt that we had something in
common. A lot of things. We were not well understood by
men; we were outcasts; and He had a sense of experience
that I felt I had. He could tell me so much about death, this
God that had spent some time with it.

When the hymn ended, Bea preached. As the service
closed, Bea asked the congregation to come to the altar and
to pray. We all did. Then Bea would come down and lay
hands on the people and pray over them, and prophesy over
them. I felt her hands press like a crown upon my head. She
started speaking in tongues. Her body shook violently. I
stared awestruck up at her, and she looked down at me. She
paused, and said she had a revelation. She looked out at the
congregation, and her hands came around and cupped my
face. She looked at me, and said that God had spoken to her
about me. She smiled and told them that God had His hands
on me, and that He was going to use me mightily in His
ministry. She swore to them, and to me, that I had been
called to God to preach. She placed her hands back on the
top of my head. "God has His hands on this boy," she told
us all. And her voice had a penetrating ring to it. A hush
hung so heavy over the congregation you could feel it. Tears
welled into my eyes. Why did I cry? I don't really know. I
was afraid, but I felt a happy weight of oncoming responsibility.

Aunt Bea looked down at me and asked me to confirm this
revelation to her God. To make her happy I nodded my head
yes. I hoped, but I wasn't sure. Shouts of "Be it so," arose
from the ecstatic congregation. Then, still holding me, Bea
said that I was to preach the next Wednesday night at prayer
meeting.

The days ran past too swiftly. I was still afraid. I had gone
over in my mind what I *wanted* to say, but what *would* I say,
and how? I had never stood in front of a group of people to
speak, except in school plays and in classes. I hated myself

for letting my aunt embarrass me into speaking in church. But I had given my word. I had to go through with it.

Behind my uncle's house, there was a large cornfield. I walked out into it, thinking of what I would say. That night I had to preach. I went to the end of the cornfield, out almost to the woods that surrounded it, opened the Bible I had brought with me, and started to preach to the cornstalks that stood like silent sentinels around me. When I spoke they nodded to me. The wind was blowing them, but it reassured me. Something was agreeing with my message, at any rate. I preached of divine love. I told the cornstalks that God loved them, that Jesus gave His life for them, died for them and arose from the dead just for them. Jesus was coming back again. If they would only accept Him as their savior, they could meet Him when He comes.

I preached of Satan, who would try to devour their souls if they were to permit it. I told them that God had set me up as a watchman of their souls. I would fight Satan with them, and I would keep the devil from them. As I spoke, I looked up and saw a large blackbird light on one of the cornstalks. The cornstalk shook, and seemed about to collapse under the weight of the bird and the force of the wind. I was sure that this was a demon from Hell. I picked up a long stick and moved stealthily to this image of Satan. I stopped and rebuked it in the name of Jesus. I pleaded the blood of Jesus to cover the cornstalk as I attacked Satan. I struck once, and then again and again. The bird flew away. I stopped. My heart beat wildly. The sweat ran down my forehead. I had succeeded only in destroying the cornstalk. It lay in ruins at my feet. Everything about it was broken. I trembled and knelt down to pick it up. I wept. Everything turned black around me. I felt like a miserable failure. Gloom and darkness enveloped me. As I closed my eyes and felt myself falling, I had the feeling of walking across a very old wooden bridge. The planks I strode upon gave way under me. I fell for a long, long time. Then I hit something soft. It was mud. I fell back into it and began to sink slowly.

I looked up through the flooring that I had broken. I could see my family looking down at me, smiling and waving goodbye. I smiled back and I waved, too. I told them that I would be all right; only death awaited. My mother told me to be good. I felt like I was drifting for a moment, then I opened my eyes. It was all changed; my cousin James was asking me if I was all right. I looked around. I was only on the ground, and the broken cornstalk was next to me. I looked at it and touched it and felt so sad. I sat up, and looked at my cousin. I told him that God had just spoken to me. He just stared at me. I got up and we walked back to the house. I still hadn't a clue as to what I was going to say.

That night the air was hot. Inside the church it was hotter still. But I felt very cold. I was scared. I was afraid of God and of my Aunt Bea. But I didn't know which one I feared more. I was scared of my cousins, the uncle and aunt I lived with and everyone in the congregation, and also of the un- known. As I sat there thinking that it couldn't get any worse, it got worse. I began to wonder what would happen if some- one brought a snake into that church, and I had to prove my faith. My feet tapped the wood of the altar floor. It was very solid.

Finally, after the prayers, the hymns and the testimonials, I was called to preach. I must have gone back to the cornfield and smote the forces of evil because later, I couldn't remem- ber a word I said that evening. But I was sure that I had preached for an eternity. It seemed never to end. Then I sat down. There were amens. I found out later that I had really talked for only four and a half minutes.

After another hymn, I stood and asked for converts. Three youths about my age, or maybe a little older, came forward. These were the first converts to accept Christ as I had ac- cepted Him. I had started, at last.

Chapter Three
Wanderlust

I had run away from my mother and brothers as a boy. I had to go back a man. I knew that before I could go home and face my mother I would have to really prove myself on my own. I had to make something out of myself to show that I was a man worthy of her respect. That way I could make up for having hurt her by running away. I knew she understood that I wasn't a coward for having left the way I did. I had written to her a lot. And she kept up a daily correspondence with me, even if it was just a postal card; I didn't always. But my relatives were constantly asking me if I remembered to drop a line to my mother. So I did write, and it wasn't too hard to do.

I wanted to go to her, but I had to make something of myself on my own first. I knew I had forced her hand by running away and not going back. And, also, I had this bug to go out West to Texas, to be with my aunt for awhile in

El Paso. I wanted to go and see the wild West, and to do some preaching. Aunt Bea had really put the bee in my bonnet. I just had to go.

My aunt in Georgia got all upset every time I mentioned it. She cried and carried on about the idea of my leaving. And she had a lot of good reasons for my not going. School. Church. Preaching. My new friends. Finally, I couldn't stand it any longer. I either had to go right away, or just forget about the whole thing. Sometimes I think that if I had hung around, I would have had to handle snakes just like Aunt Bea did. I didn't want to. And I still don't.

To add to the pressure I was under, my aunt in El Paso sent me the money for the ticket. And I bought the ticket. And I told her I had. Then she kept pestering me to tell her when to meet the bus.

I had to talk to my aunt and uncle and cousins and friends, and to Auntie Bea. I told her that I wanted to try preaching in a new place. And she said, "Boy, you go right ahead." Well, pretty soon I had everybody persuaded to my way of thinking. Finally, they all gave me their blessings, and I could really set my departure date. My uncle gave me his black suit. I was really coming up fast, and it fit me just perfectly. I was so proud of it. It had a black vest. And my uncle gave me a pocket watch. I sure looked like some dude.

I had a strange sense of freedom as I went to Texas. I had some ideas on religion that I wanted to try out. I was lonesome for our old home. I missed my father. I really grieved for him. But I knew I couldn't go back. The old life just wasn't there anymore. I wanted to find a way to work it all out. I don't know, even now, what I expected to find. I think it was a big unknown just beckoning me on. I knew I'd see my father's sister. She had lived in Tallahassee. She was the only girl in my father's family, and they all treated her like something special. I think that's why she never really got along well with my mother. But she had been in Tallahassee when my father was killed. She was visiting there with her four children. She had three girls and a boy.

Finally, I left. I told my people out in Texas that I was on my way. And everybody went to the depot to see me off. That bus trip seems to me like one of the longest I have ever taken. I was sure I had been in Texas for over a month, and El Paso was nowhere in sight.

But finally there it was. I stepped off the bus, and there were my aunt and all of her kids waiting for me. I threw my arms around them all. We were so happy we cried. And a funny thing happened. Through my tears I saw snow for the first time in my life. It scared me. I couldn't figure out what it was that made the ground so white. Then, when they told me, I just couldn't get over it. Sure, that was the stuff I'd been reading about in the school books. And here it was real.

I liked El Paso. It was big. It had so many different things going on. It snowed. It got hot. It got dusty. It got dry. It was windy. And all of that happened in the same season of the year, in winter. What kind of crazy place had I really come to?

We all attended a little Pentecostal school next to the church. It was right across the street from a large Catholic school for unwed mothers. These girls fascinated me, so, when I was asked to preach in that little church, I preached about the wages of sin. And I would look towards that big Catholic school across the street, kind of roll my eyes and grin. And everyone knew just what I was talking about, too.

Everybody liked me. And I liked everybody. I sure kept busy with school, preaching and all. But I worried about mother, my brothers and things back in Florida and Georgia. I was homesick. I kept my homesickness under control for a long time, but it kept eating away at me, and getting worse. My mother's letters would make me just long to get back on that bus and return to Florida. Mother's letters got more and more insistent. Then, pretty soon, telegrams began to come from her. I knew I had promised to go, but I knew I still wasn't ready. I hadn't proved myself enough—not yet. So, I hung on for a time. But Mother couldn't wait. She needed her family together, and she let everyone know about it.

One telegram said to my aunt, "I'm going to have you arrested, if you don't send Troy back home." She was getting pretty close to the end of her rope. My aunt just felt all was well, nothing to worry about, just let Mother try to have an arrest made.

But I wanted to go home. I told my aunt that. She understood. I remember, when it came down to it, I just said, "Well, I'll go on home now, if you all don't mind." And there were goodbyes all around, and I left. I had such mixed feelings. I had been happy there. El Paso was big and exciting, and it had given me the urge to travel. I still have that urge.

Yet, I couldn't wait to get back home to Florida. That was really home to me. Mother had a little house in Winter Haven. She had done a lot in the time I had been away. She had emerged with such strength. She had kept all of my brothers in school, except the smallest ones. They were too young. And she managed to take care of them while she worked. She had added a new role—that of breadwinner—to those of housewife and mother. So she had set herself up in Winter Haven, and she was making it all work out for herself and her children.

I had quite a homecoming. We were all so close. It seems to me, even now, that love and faith held us all together. We all relied so heavily on each other for help and guidance and love.

This attitude strengthened us in our faith in God, and in our reliance on each other. And we needed it. Things were very hard for us. When Dad was alive we all lived on easy street. Now, we were fighting poverty. I had a job after school, and as my little brothers got old enough, so did they. We all did whatever we could to help our mother.

We had moved to Auburndale for a time, and we were still shifting about, rootless. We finally ended up in Mobile, Alabama. There we all experienced the pressures of poverty in a big city for the first time.

Relatives came and wanted to split up the family. I think

a split would have killed my mother. She had fought through so much to get her family together and to hold it together. She was a fierce fighter; she still is. The easy thing for her would have been to give up. Things were really rough. We didn't have food in the house sometimes during that period. Mother tried working for wages, too.

The kind of work she could do was pretty limited. She was a little old country girl, with only a tenth grade education. That was as high as the school went, and that's as high as she had ever gone. But she had no special skills. She had scarcely ever worked for wages, and then only as a fruit packer during the season in one of the Florida packing plants. That was after the failure of her third marriage. She had worked as a housewife all her life. She was essentially a wife and mother. And believe me, I know that that's a real career all by itself. But, when you add to that being a bread-winner, it can be really rough. Mobile presented a different and tougher situation than she'd ever been in. We were all in school. We all did whatever odd jobs we could do to bring in a little extra money. But it just wasn't enough. Mother even went to work as a B-girl in a bar, just to keep us all together—to keep her body and soul together—and I mean that literally, and in the sense of the preservation of her family. I'm sure she had to do a lot of things that she's not proud of, but she kept her family intact.

I remember one time, my mother told me that she had stayed up all night worrying about what she was going to feed us for breakfast. She didn't think there was enough food in the house. You see, I'd brought a friend home from school, and he stayed over at our place. When we got up, there was breakfast. Mother had found some flour some-place, and made pancakes. We bolted them down and ran off to school. That's the kind of security and affection that surrounded us.

Keeping us all together shows the kind of real strength she has. We were down and out, but we held together. And I'll never forget those days. My brothers and I learned a lot from it. Nothing would ever drive us apart after that. And we have certainly been tested in that respect. I think that's one reason why my brothers stood by me, without any question, when the whole thing about my being a gay minister came out. It was the strength and sureness of a silent communication that had fired our souls way back there in Mobile. It still inspires all of us every day. And, I mean to let you know that my brothers and I take care of our mother today. There are people who would tell you that a homosexual is overly attached to his mother—too fondly so. I don't feel that I am. I just have a good memory now for recalling those times, when we were coming up. We were too small, and too selfishly growing in our own ways to realize the way she slaved for us. Well, now we do realize. I have her with me, now, as much as I can, because I want to repay a debt that I've owed her for such a long time. I owe her my life, and so do my brothers owe her theirs. We're just saying thank you in our own way. We always respected our parents. Respect was as sacred a thing in our home as it was in the old Chinese homes, and in the Old Testament homes. We were involved in our home. We loved and respected our parents because we wanted to. And they certainly returned that love and respect.

One of the ways I helped out at home was by preaching. I didn't make much money at it, and in addition, I had to work as a stock boy in dime stores, or do whatever I could to help make ends meet. But I loved preaching. I had preached regularly since Aunt Bea permitted me to preach in Georgia.

When I was fifteen I got my license to preach. The procedure is fairly simple. One just goes before a congregation and preaches a sermon. Then, at the next regular business meeting of the church administration, the application for the license is included for consideration on the agenda. A license gives one the right to preach. But all the other ministerial and pastoral functions must wait for ordination. That takes place after one successfully completes a course of study at a Bible college. But my first license was granted by the Baptist church that we attended in Winter Haven.

Even in junior high, I had preached at least once a week. I held chapel services every Tuesday morning. It gave me a real feeling of exhilaration. I knew I was doing the right thing. This is what I really wanted to do. One thing I felt sure of: God had called me to preach.

This same desire to preach continued on into high school. In Mobile I went to Murphy High School. I attended Tolmanville Baptist Church, one of the largest such churches in Mobile. But even though I liked the people, I felt that there was something lacking.

I was convinced that the something I lacked was a girl friend. So I got one. Her father was the pastor of the Prichard Church of God. I went there with her. I got to know everybody. I preached. And the Lord blessed real, real good. It was a church with a lot of social activity. It was just great. It seemed to me to be just fantastic, everything I had ever wanted. My girl friend, and my affiliation with the Pentecostal church gave an added zest to the emotional charge I got out of religion, out of communion with God and out of being in touch with everybody. I had turned away from the Baptist church. But you see, I think I was already secretly, deep down, turning away from a heterosexual life. Had I maintained that orientation, I would have made it in the white Anglo-Saxon Protestant religious area. Maybe that's only a dream, or a fantasy of what might have been. But, as I look back, I think I was being prepared then for the mission I have now, where I am so much better off.

Then there was a kind of three-way tug of war always going on inside of me. Pulling one way was the physical world. That was the world of the senses. It was a world of sensual pleasure and sensual pain. It was a real mystery to me. My daily experiences of the nature of my body, of desire, of sexual fantasies, of intense emotional feeling, of reaction to the physical world was a real set of problems that I had to live with and cope with. Sometimes I felt elated.

Then again, I would feel depressed. I would feel great guilt at my heterosexual desires, or at my homosexual leanings. I just couldn't understand the drives. I also had the world of metaphysics and mysticism that I felt as a real, living, almost physical presence. And, too, I had the world of God, and of past history, the sense of being in transit through this life from others and to others. These forces were like physical tugs that went round and round inside me, pulling here and there. I actually felt it all, and tried to have the spiritual dominate me. I strove for perfection. And the more I tried, the more elusive it was.

I was beset by self-doubts. Everyone who thinks he has a religious calling is. They never really go away. But the realization grows and you finally know that's it. You are often tried very severely, and tested sorely in bringing yourself into a working alignment with your mission in life. I've even been in jail for mine. I may be there again; I don't know.

I do know that at age sixteen along with my doubts about everything, and with the need to find myself in all ways, I had guilt feelings about any sexual urges. I think I wanted to know how others felt. I wanted to know, I had to know, what the other boys were doing about it. That curiosity drove me to more experimentation with homosexuality. I kept asking, "Why me, God? Now, why, God, did you call me, and yet I have these feelings? Why do I have these attractions to a fellow?" I had the conflict between my feelings and what the church taught. I would ask God about it in prayers. I remember then, I would say, "Well, now, why God, would you let me have those feelings even before I knew I was called to preach?"

In Mobile I had found another branch of the Church of God, and I became very heavily involved in it. But I still felt awful. I went through a terrible time, and I was always asking the Lord to really come to me, and help me, and not to let me masturbate, or have those strong sexual feelings. It was a real struggle. And I wasn't very successful at coping.

My feelings were just too strong, and I discharged my tensions however I could.

I remember that summer in 1956, when I was just sixteen. I went to a youth camp run by the Pentecostal Church. There was a large group of boys there, and we experimented. The state youth director didn't know anything about what was going on. And I was the biggest boy there. I was tall for my age, and somewhat oversized, so I was the leader. Most of the rest were from about fourteen and a half to sixteen. But to make matters worse, I didn't have any relatives who were members of the church. Most of the kids there were P. K.'s (preacher's kids). Well, when the experimentation was whispered around, who do you suppose became the scapegoat in all of it? Why, Troy Perry, of course.

The state youth director came up to see me and said, "Is it true that you touched John . . . you know where?" Well, I was so shocked, I turned as white as a sheet. I broke up, and I bawled and cried. Finally, I said, "Well, we were just playing and having a good time."

He said, "Well, you go to your cabin. I'm going to send you home."

That just broke my heart. I thought that God had really let me down. I went back to my cabin. I found out that the same thing had happened to one of the other boys that I ran into on his way to his cabin. We also found out who told, because he was sent to his cabin. He felt worse because he had betrayed us. They didn't send us home because camp was over the next day, but I didn't think about how idle the threat had been right then.

The next day our pastors came to pick us up. The youth director said to mine, "Something happened with Troy. But it's not important. Don't worry about it."

The pastor didn't press any points. But, when we got home, he put his son, James, up to asking me to come over to his house so I could spend the night. He wanted to know if anything would happen. I was so dumb. James asked me, and I asked the pastor, "Is it all right if I come over and spend the night at your house? James wants me to." He was very jolly as he reassured me that it would be just fine.

The next morning, they quizzed James about the night. Had Troy touched him, or done anything? And James said, "Oh, no. Troy wouldn't do anything." Well, I lucked out. James wasn't my type, and I really hadn't done anything at all.

But that didn't end the whole thing. We had an organization in our church called the Lamp Lighters. It was similar to the Boy Scouts. It was an honor organization for boys in the Pentecostal Church. And you moved up the ladder as you went along through the studies that this group had to do.

No one had ever won the Silver Flame, which was the highest award you could ever attain. There were no Silver Lamp Lighters in the whole state. Well, I was determined that I was going to win it. And I did. I memorized all the stuff. All the goodies. And I could whip through it like nobody's business.

The leader at our church was so elated he called the general headquarters. General headquarters was just tickled to death. They told him to call the state youth director and tell him about it and ask him to verify it. After that verification, the state youth director would send in the word, and they would run a big story in the church papers about the first person in the church to win the Silver Flame. Prior to that, there had been a lot of needling in the church papers to the effect of, "All right, Kiddies, when is somebody going to win the Silver Flame? Don't be dodoes!" Well, my award had been verified by three ministers who had me memorize all the teachings of the church, and the Bible scriptures, and the thirty doctrinal points.

I was so proud. They were so proud. And it had been announced in church. Then came the cold water. The state youth director said, "Absolutely no! He can't have that award. I disqualify him. If I give him that award, I'm going to have ministers down my neck. One of the boy's fathers from camp wants me to excommunicate him. How would all of these people react? The answer has to be a permanent no. And I don't want to hear anymore about it."

That really broke my heart. I had tried so hard, and I had won it. And then to lose by some kind of default, I just couldn't understand it. So I cried and carried on for days with the pastor of the church and with the men in the church. They wanted to know if I was really going to be totally ruined for life by not getting the award. Well, I felt as if I might just go ahead and be upset for that long. I felt that as long as I stayed in that church, and as long as everyone remembered that incident, it would follow me for the rest of my life. But I finally thought, well, if that's the way it is, then that's the way it's got to be. It was a hard experience, but I finally accepted the fact that I wouldn't get that award.

But that church pulled all of their youth group out of the Lamp Lighters to protest against the state organization, and the state youth director. The local people felt that the award should have been made on merit, and they stood by me in that. Their attitude was that they didn't care what I had done or been accused of; I had earned the award, and I should have had it.

Well, again I turned inward, and I berated myself for my feelings. I tried to suppress them. I preached more and harder. I turned to girls. But nothing really worked. I knew that somewhere, somehow my strong physical attraction for the masculine image that I carried with me would find an answering reflection. And I kind of went along day to day waiting for it to happen. And once in awhile it did. It was like those experimentations. I felt more a man afterwards. And so, reassured, I could turn again to girls. It was a strange cycle.

So, until I was eighteen, things went along as kind of a blur. I felt things locking into place. I thought I could make a bisexual accommodation, or be a semiheterosexual, as one of my friends now describes it. Many people have done so.

I think more homosexuals are living a semiheterosexual existence than otherwise. I know their problems. I had them. But for a minister, a man of the cloth, it is almost impossible.

I didn't know what kind of accommodation I could make. But I felt that I could. I just didn't know enough about myself, nor about my sexual makeup. But I met the girl that I was sure was for me. Marriage looked like the best deal all around, and it would be the easy way out.

Chapter Four
The Bonds
of Matrimony

At age seventeen I followed the course set out for any Southern young man who decides that he wants to be a man of the cloth. I looked around for the woman who would share my life as a minister's wife. I knew it would be hard. She'd have to scrimp and save, and live a fairly poor life with me until I was through with Bible college and ordination. Even then, it wouldn't be easy. Most Pentecostal preachers have to work a full day in a white-collar job, if they can find one, so that they can spend their "free" time preaching. This is true even after ordination. Once in awhile you hit it lucky and get a rich congregation that can afford to pay you a good salary. But for years, that was the exception, not the rule. Of course, that picture is changing all the time, so the secular side of being a man of God is getting to be a fairly good thing. It's getting to be easier all the time.

It all fit into the scheme of things. I went to a church

service, and the girl who played the piano lit the spark. She was pretty, she had a winning smile, and she had a mind of her own. That was all for me.

And, selfishly, I must admit that every minister needs a piano player. That attracted me. But when I talked to her I was really attracted. She said what she thought. Sometimes that embarrassed her family, but they respected her for her opinions. Everyone did. She worked hard. She did a lot of church work. But she didn't hold much with the forms of religions. She was never the zealot I was. If she didn't want to go to the altar to pray people "through," as we say, she wouldn't. We pray people through crisis, illness and moral difficulties. Of course, she never questioned the church. She had been raised in it. She was a member. But she did her religious work and worship her own way, not Troy Perry's, nor anyone else's. But all of these qualities really attracted me to her.

We saw a lot of each other for about three months, and then I popped the question. We became engaged, and we were engaged for just about nine months before we were married. We were both eighteen when we married, and we turned nineteen soon afterwards. She never changed after we were married. She was just the same. I'm sure she still is today.

I had the impression from our church that you had to marry to be ordained. And in our Southern society we were taught that the only life style is the heterosexual one. There is just nothing else. Of course, the homosexual style is practiced quietly, secretly and constantly by a large segment. It is kind of known, but never spoken of. Meanwhile, one is pushed toward marriage and having children. Everyone is supposed to give his mother grandchildren, and share in the happiness that brings her. If you loved someone, and felt like marrying, that was the thing to do. It was better to marry than to burn, as St. Paul had pointed out. That helped me make up my mind to become engaged and to go ahead and marry.

At that point I felt that I was successfully suppressing my homosexuality. I didn't want to be a "queer," whatever that was. And that was the word, the language, that was used for anyone who had any feeling for members of the same sex. And I hadn't played around with anyone, with any other fellow, for a long time. I thought I had it licked.

I know that there were pressures building up in me as the marriage date approached. Also, I had been licensed by the Pentecostal group. They hadn't been very enthusiastic about taking me on, but I had my Baptist license, and I think they thought I wasn't settled in. I had been in Florida, Georgia, Texas, Alabama, and it seemed like I might just take off. I think, too, that some may have heard about our youth camp the year before. I'm not sure. But they became convinced that I would straighten out as soon as I got married. So they went ahead and licensed me. I planned to go to Chicago to attend Bible college.

Then, a friend of my wife's showed up—I'll call him John. He'd been kind of a boy friend or a friend boy. He was delighted that Gloria, my fiancée, and I were fixing to get hitched. He took to hanging around with both of us a lot. He was gay, but he wasn't obvious about it. One night he just showed up and spent the night with me. And that was it. Every night we were together, and here I was dating Gloria. So he said, "Well, when you marry Gloria, this has got to stop."

And I said, "Oh, I agree with you one hundred percent." In the back of our minds we were both wondering what she would say if she found out. John was kind of a shirt-tail relative of Gloria's family, so he kind of popped in and out of their lives.

I got married! And I turned over a new leaf. Wham! I broke off my relationship with John. I packed up my wife and moved to Chicago and went right into Bible college. I was determined to make it all work.

The course I entered in Bible college was one of my greatest challenges. I loved it. I was as enthusiastic about studying the mysteries and miracles of the Bible, of the whole ancient world as I have been about anything else in my life. It just seemed to come to life for me. It was hard work, and it kept me busy. The students were all close to each other. I felt drawn to them, and they were drawn to me. I was asked to run for vice president of the student government. Election was a snap.

Everything ran along smoothly for about two months. Then some fellow I'd known in Mobile, named Richie, showed up. I'd never bedded him, but there he was in Chicago determined to go to bed with me. He kept insisting that he had a really mad crush on me.

I felt pretty safe. But I had a sister-in-law living in Chicago, and she called up, wanting to know how our Mobile visitor was, and where he was staying. "If he doesn't have any place to stay, why doesn't he stay there tonight with Troy, and Gloria can come over and spend the night with me. That way you won't have to sleep on the couch." And that's the way it was. Gloria said sure, and I went along with it all, but I was scared. It had been over two months since I'd touched another man, and he was the first fellow I'd ever met who openly admitted that he was a homosexual. He hung the label on himself and said that was just the way it was.

That night he tried to have sex with me. I was so scared, I had a pretty frantic and restless night. The next day he left, and I was sure relieved, but the adventure and the anxiety surrounding his visit kind of excited me. If Glorida sensed anything, she never let on.

About a week later, the F.B.I. came to the door looking for Richie. It seems that the young man was a commercial artist for a firm. He had cashed two checks for this firm, big checks, totaling around $13,000. The bank knew him because he often did that. He was a trusted staff member. He told the bank that his father, who owned the firm, had died, and he needed to get these checks cashed. So the bank complied. He had waited around for about three days to take delivery of a new specially ordered Ford car. It was the kind with the retractable hard top. It was a beauty, and he had a lot of special gadgets on it. The F.B.I. was looking for that car and its driver. They never asked anything about his being a homosexual. I just said that he's spent the night with us, and that he'd gone on, and we didn't know where. They thanked us, and left to continue their search.

Things had just settled down when my in-laws dropped by for a visit. John, my last bachelor romance, was driving their car for them. He was very helpful to all of us in so many ways. Gloria and I told them about our young caller from Mobile, the Ford, the checks and the visit from the F.B.I. Yes, they said, it was true. He was wanted. But that wasn't the end of it. When he could get me alone, John wanted to know more. He was jealous and he was mad. He knew that I had spent the night with the visitor. Gloria had mentioned that rather offhandedly. But John was so upset. He let me know that he was in love with me. Well, this was all very foreign to me. Two men just didn't love each other in that way. And the whole idea of male jealousy was something I just couldn't understand. I put him off. I said that I was busy. I was. I had school, my job, and I was pastoring a little church in Joliet, Illinois.

In that church we were in the midst of a building fund campaign, and that took all the energy and time we could put into it. It was a small Pentecostal church that I loved with all my heart.

But in the middle of this campaign, and just after the visits, we had a two-week vacation coming up. So Gloria and I drove back to Florida to visit my people. We had just gotten there, and it seemed as if we turned right around and came back.

When I got back I called the district overseer and said, "Hi, this is Troy. And we're back in town, and ready to hit the ball again."

He asked me, "Where are you at, right now?"

"Well, we're here visiting Sister Elizabeth's."

"I've got to see you. Don't leave there."

"Well, I was just going over to the church. Why don't I meet you over there?"

"That's fine. And you know, Troy, the state overseer's here, too."

So they came down, and I met them at the church, and we went walking in. They went up front and looked at the growing number of congregation members that we had marked on our plaque.

The state overseer looked pleased and said, "It sure looks like you're growing!"

I reassured them and said, "Yes, the Lord's blessing real, real good." But something was wrong. I could feel the tension.

He turned around and looked at me and said, "I think you *know* what I'm here for."

I had that sinking feeling inside. I knew. I just knew. I said, "Yes, I think I do." My mouth was all dry. I knew that John had talked. I felt it somehow. It was the first time I ever felt the destructive, sick revenge of a jealous lover. It just blew my mind.

So the man said, "How quick can you leave?" Just that way.

"I'm not sure. I really don't know. We don't have any money. We just came back from our vacation."

"I want you to go right back to Florida. There's going to be a lot of talk around here."

I felt so dirty. That's why I hate the word queer so much. I felt the crushing stigma of being known as a queer. It hurt then. Now it wouldn't. I have a perfect defense against that kind of cruelty, but then, it was on a plane so revolting that no one could talk about it, nor even pray about it. Not once did they say, "Can we pray for you?"—nothing except, "How quick can you get out of town?" I was so bowled over. But it wasn't finished by any means.

The state overseer said, "Does your wife know anything at all about this?"

"No, not at all."

Well, you know how tough you have to be to make it to state overseer. He said, "Do you want me to call her?"

"No, sir, I'll talk to my wife myself." And, I went out, drove off, and by the time I picked Gloria up I was crying. She wanted to know what had happened. I just couldn't tell her, then. I took her to our house. It was completely furnished, and I told her we had to leave and go back to Florida right away.

Gloria looked at me searchingly and said, "Why?"

I fumbled around for an answer. Finally I said, "I just can't tell you." There was a long pause.

"Well, I'm not sure I'm going anywhere," she said. "I want to go up to my family's, now, please." Her whole family was there in Chicago, including John. I told her that the overseer had given me the money to go back home, but she had to go and say goodbye to her family. She wanted me to come in with her, but I just couldn't.

I dropped her off, and said, "I'm not going in there. I'm going to give you an hour to talk to them. And then I'll be back." She went in, and I drove off. I rode over to a part of Chicago that I didn't know. I just parked the car and sat there. I never felt so low in all my life. I was just totally defeated, and betrayed, and I couldn't cope with this problem. I didn't know what to do, nor which way to turn.

When the hour was up, I drove back, sounded the horn and picked Gloria up. She said, "Well, I talked to Mom and them. They all expected me to stay there. And I told them that I love you, and I'm going with you. And that we'll work things out." She'd been crying; I could see that. She said, "I know what it's all about. When I was there John came in. He'd been drinking. He's wild. He loves you and wants you, but he'll destroy you." She looked at me, and added, "I don't understand any of this, Troy. Please explain it to me. Please!"

Well, I couldn't. I didn't understand it myself. I could only say, "I can't. I don't want to talk about it." It was just a bad scene.

We drove almost nonstop from Illinois to Florida. We got back to my mother's in jig time. Mother was pretty surprised to see us again so soon. But even though she knew something was wrong, she said, "Well, you took us up on the offer to move back to Florida, I see." And she kept it on that level. She never pried. I marvel that she didn't, because we must have looked pretty dragged out after the trip and in our emotional state.

We had to find housing. I had to get a job, and I had to figure things out about myself and religion—where to turn. Well, I went looking for a job. And it wasn't all that easy in that neck of the woods. Finally, I did get one. That made things easier around the house. I kept busy so I wouldn't have to explain anything, but it didn't ease the tension.

I worried about going to church. I couldn't get over the loneliness I felt, being out of it all. How could the church not pray for me? I felt that they had let me down. My wife and I had things patched up, but we hadn't really resolved anything. We needed to know more about each other, and more about my sexual dilemma.

One evening I came in from work, and my wife had been crying again. I asked her what was the matter. She said, "Oh, I got a letter from my sister in Chicago." I asked her what was in the letter. Gloria said, "She had plenty to say. Just listen to this. . . ." She started reading the letter. It was one of the nastiest letters I've ever heard. She started in on how dirty and filthy I was. She was even describing some of the sex acts that had gone on. I grabbed that letter out of my wife's hand, and I just stared at it, as if it wasn't real. My wife went right on; she could quote that letter from memory. I don't know what snapped in me, but I slapped her. I'd never hit a woman before in my life, and I was stunned to realize that I had just slapped my wife. I guess I was pretty close to a nervous breakdown. I was so enraged at my sister-in-law. I just wondered, my God, how can that woman do this? The things she'd written and said, and kept repeating. It made me feel dirty all over.

I don't know whether John had taken off on his own, or been tossed out, but he was out of it. I know they gave him a pretty rough time, too. Now, I know that he had his reasons for what he did. However bad I felt, I did find it in my heart to forgive him, because I knew the agony he must have been suffering.

I started going to the little church in Lake Alford, and I became the assistant pastor. Then the church split into two segments. I stayed there and pastored at Lake Alford. It was a pretty little rural church. Gloria and I got a piano that we gave to the church. I think it's still there. Things quieted down. We had our first boy, and everything seemed to be going along just fine.

I had made one mistake, however. I was determined not to be exposed again as I had been in Joliet. So, when I became the assistant pastor I took the pastor into my confidence and told him what had happened. His attitude was, "Oh well, when I was younger things like that happened. So don't worry about it." But that was a mistake I would advise everyone to avoid. I regretted it soon afterwards. When our churches split and I became his rival instead of his assistant, he started a little whispering campaign. What I had done was as stupid as handing someone a loaded pistol.

What I hadn't realized when I'd spilled my story was that there was a witch hunt going on throughout Florida. It came about through the Johns Commission, appointed by the state legislature to investigate and to root out homosexuality in Florida, and to expose it. Mr. Johns, who headed the commission, was later appointed governor. His appointment filled a vacancy created by a death. Florida doesn't have a lieutenant governor, so the governor is appointed by the state legislature, whenever a governor's death occurs. Johns and his people published a pamphlet called "Homosexuality and Citizenship in Florida." It was an exposé. The commission's members revealed their stupidity by having two thou-

sand illustrated copies of their report printed. It was to go
to school children and the general public. Among the illus-
trations were photos of two men performing fellatio on each
other, and a police photo of one man committing fellatio on
another in a public rest room. The report was recalled and
quickly suppressed, but the witch hunt intensified.

I was still so dumb, I hadn't read anything about homosexuality or homosexuals. I didn't even know about the
Johns Commission report.

But, as a result of that report, the slightest breath of scandal about homosexuality could ruin a person, forever. In our
county, alone, over 150 people had left. These were prominent people. Some were driven to committing suicide. There
was a wave of that. These people were called up in front of
judges and asked about homosexual acts and homosexual
people they knew. It was just like the Spanish Inquisition.
People with well-established jobs or from prominent families, just disappeared. And this was in 1961.

One member of my congregation came to me in private
and said, "You better be careful what you say or do around
here. Your rival is going to have you down in front of the
judge." Inside I knew that what was being said was probably
true. But I felt powerless to do anything about it. I couldn't
make another admission.

But I had to. I had told my people at Lake Alford that I
was thinking about going back to school to finish Bible
college. Then something happened that forced the issue.
Actually, I was going to take a church in Leesburg, Florida
first.

Someone sent a letter from the state church office to my
wife. Since Gloria and my mother were such close friends,
she called and my mother rushed over, and this was her
reaction:

"I didn't know anything at all about the homosexual life.
Not until Troy. Oh, I knew there was such a thing, but it
never crossed my mind. I guess I just never was aware of it.
I never recognized any sign of it. In fact, as I think about it,

I know I didn't. I just had a very traditional reaction. That was my attitude. But then it hit close to home. And when it did, and I found out, it like to have knocked me off my feet.

"It was a revelation to me—finding out that way—having my own son accused. Because, here he was married, and with a baby and all. And I just didn't believe it. I couldn't.

"Troy and his wife lived close to me there in central Florida. He had a job to support himself and his family. And that way he could preach and do his church work.

"It happened. His wife called me and said that there was a letter there that I should read. She and I were good friends —real close. She sounded so strange. I knew that something was wrong—bad wrong. I could tell by the strained way she sounded on the telephone. And, I went right over. I asked her what could have upset her so much. Well, she didn't say anything at all. She just handed me this letter. It had been sent to her from the state overseer of their church. It was addressed to both of them. But that man knew that she'd see it first. He knew that Troy worked during the day and wouldn't be home until the afternoon, sometime after the mail was delivered. And he knew that she worked right along in the church with Troy, and would surely open any church letters that came along.

"Well, the letter was about Troy. Troy and some other young man. And I read it. And I had to sit down. Then she said she had a suspicion that it might be true. That really took the wind out of me. We just sat there looking like a couple of gravediggers, and Troy walked in on us like that. Well, by that time I was so mad I just couldn't hardly stand it.

"Troy said, 'You two are sitting there like two vultures, ready to pounce on me. What's wrong?' Then he read the letter. Tears came into his eyes. I asked him right off if there was anything to it. I started to cry, because I didn't know a thing about it.

"I said, 'Troy, I'm not trying to hurt; I'm trying to find

out.' I wanted to get a lawyer and make the person prove the things he was saying in the letter that Troy was. Well, I guess when Troy came in and saw us sitting there, he must have known. I guess, like all gay men and women, he knew that one day his family, those closest to him, would know. It was an awful moment for all of us.

"Troy looked at me real hard and said, 'No, Mother, you all are against me!'

"And I said, 'No, son, I'm not. But what I am saying is I'd get a lawyer and we'll make him prove these things.'

"Troy said, 'No, Mother, not with this thing, this witch hunt going on.' You see, it was 1961, and there had been a real witch hunt in Florida. Many people were being exposed, and having their lives ruined. Some left. Some killed themselves. Even if nothing was proven, just being accused was enough.

"Then, Troy looked at me deep and searching, and he said, 'I can't fight it, because it's true.' And that's how I found out, found out that he was homosexual.

"It was a shock to me, because it had never crossed my mind. I grew, finally, to accept it. Of course, there was a lot of water that had to pass under the bridge before that time. But I think if any mother has that to face, then it is a real test of her own love for her children. And, if she really loves them, it won't matter. Not in the long run. If ever my son needed just lots of love, and sympathy, and understanding —and no questions asked—that was the time. And that's the way it was.

"He and his wife went on and lived together. And we just kind of forgot all about it. I thought he knew whatever it was would have to be worked out, in his own way, in his own time and in his own life. And so things went along just like always, at least on the surface."

And so it was—on the surface. But inside I was really up-tight. I thought that people were looking at me suspiciously, even out on the street. I kept saying to myself, "I'm not a homosexual." It was just so foreign to me.

The congregation in Leesburg was an independent one. It was not in the Church of God, and I snapped at it. So we went on up there, running away to another new beginning. But I also carried along with me my homosexuality, which I had not even begun to explore.

I worked hard. I had a job right off. And I had a marvelous congregation. By the time I was twenty-one, I was the assistant state overseer of the Emmanuel Holiness Church, and ordained. I was young, but I had proven my ability. And everyone felt that it was just my dish. I had demonstrated my good common sense. And this congregation, this whole church, had never heard one breath of scandal about me. As close as all the churches were, nothing was ever said. It was a kind of fellowship that didn't admit that anything like homosexuality could be the case. I pastored there in Leesburg for six months. But I had to finish my schooling. And there were other things bugging me, too. I wanted to go back to Illinois. I had to go back and square everything away. I wanted to either purge myself of my "guilt," or avenge myself for the sense of wrong I had. I needed to let everyone know that I had made restitution. That was the Pentecostal way of doing things.

So I did go back to Illinois. I enrolled in night classes at the Moody Bible Institute. I got a job, and I settled in. Then I went over to the headquarters church at Summit, Illinois. That was the Church of God that I had attended. But the same district overseer was there. It was restitution time, so I went in, and I pleaded and prayed, and cried for an hour. But I got no help whatsoever. If you were excommunicated from a congregation for homosexual reasons, you were never to be reinstated. So my wife and I attended our neighborhood church, and quietly prayed and waited.

Then, one Sunday, some people from a rival church came to ours. These people were from the Church of God of Prophecy. I'd never even thought about another congregation, nor another church. They said, "You've got to come over and visit our church one time."

I smiled and said, "I'd like to." And the next week I did. I just fell in love with those people. It was so pleasant, and so like the Church of God. It was a sect that had split from the Church of God in 1923, so it was almost parallel to it. The doctrine was exactly the same. I transferred my membership. I was still running from my homosexuality. I didn't want to be a queer, whatever that was. I just wanted to preach. Everything was great. I preached in that church. And the Lord anointed. He brought people in to hear me preach. And they supported that church enthusiastically.

My job with a plastics firm was going great guns, too. One day the director of operations came over and said that they were opening a new plant in Torrance, California. They needed someone who knew their operation and could be really helpful as a junior executive. He wanted to know if I was interested. I said, "Sure. No problem. I'd like to go out there."

So I said goodbye to the congregation. I think in the back of my mind I knew that someday the rivals at my former church would be over to make sure I was ousted.

The plastic company paid all my expenses to move out west. I packed up the family and came out to California. No sweat. I had kept my nose clean. During that long stretch in Illinois I hadn't looked twice at another man. It looked as if everything would be fine. I felt like it anyway.

I settled in California and went right to work. I wrote the state overseer of the Church of God of Prophecy to see if there might be a local opening for a minister in any of our congregations. A church in Santa Ana was looking for a pastor. So I applied. They looked me over, and I was in. I started preaching. I was a pastor of my own flock. As soon as I started, people started coming to church. They wanted to hear me preach. We all trod the straight and narrow. No deviation from doctrine. No movies. No dancing. No smoking. No drinking. No nothing.

Time sped by. I was already twenty-three. I was pastoring my own church and doing very well. To all appearances I was a very happy individual. But inwardly I felt a lack of something. I felt unfulfilled. There was something that I wasn't really sure about. Something about my past kept bothering me. It was like a recurring itch. I was sure that I had completely suppressed my homosexual feelings. I didn't want to be bothered by them any more. Homosexuality was wrong. So my church kept telling me, over and over again. And I read the Scriptures, and I kept on literally interpreting as we Pentecostals do. It was always the same. Homosexuality was wrong—dead wrong. Being a queer was the most horrible thing in American society. It was the last thing in the world I wanted to be.

Still I had that strange feeling. Something was lacking. Something was wrong. I needed something else. What was it? I didn't know. Or I wouldn't let myself know. Life suddenly seemed to be passing me by—racing. I felt uneasy and very restless. Part of the reason was that now I had a second son. My wife had to take the baby home for an extended vacation to Alabama and Illinois to show him off to all of the relatives. So she took both children and went.

I always liked to make some topical reference to current affairs in my sermons. So one day, while my wife was gone, I did the usual thing, I went into any handy bookstore to buy one of the national news magazines. But when I walked up to the cash register to pay for it, my eye caught some male physique magazines enticingly displayed there. Well, I paused and looked at them. I could never even remember having seen any physique magazines in my life. I paused and browsed. The provocative poses and positions that those males assumed really turned me on. And that was back in the old days, when they were all still wearing bathing suits or posing briefs. I really studied those books. I was there so long I was embarrassed to leave, and embarrassed to buy them. Finally, I realized that I was being stared at by the management. So I finally went up to the woman behind the counter, and said to her, "Tell me something. Do you have any books on homosexuality?" That was a hard word for me to get out.

She was very courteous. She smiled at me, and said, "Yes, we do have a few."

I took the bull by the horns, and said, "Well, give me a copy of everything you've got."

She made up a package of paperbacks and magazines, and I wrote out a check for $32.17. I think I still have that cancelled check stuck away somewhere. I took the bag of reading matter home, and in the quietness of the parsonage, I started reading—really studying. The novels didn't tell me anything that I wanted to know. Sure, they did turn me on a bit, but not much. I needed some really factual material. I turned to *The Homosexual In America,* by Donald Webster Cory. When I finished the book, I knew without the shadow of a doubt that I was a homosexual; I was gay. And there was just nothing for me to be afraid of any longer. This was it. I could honestly look at myself in the mirror, and say to myself, "You know something, you're a homosexual." And it didn't upset me.

There was a magazine that the woman had dropped into the bag. It was called *ONE,* and it was published by One, Incorporated, probably the oldest homophile organization in America. When I read it, I learned that there were millions of other homosexuals all across America, and that they were often as confused as I was. I learned of some of the problems, some of the research, and about the attitudes and pressures brought to bear on the whole field of homosexuality. When I read these books and articles, a burden seemed to be lifted from my shoulders. I put the books and magazines aside, and thought about them for a time. Then I reread everything, and finally, I read Cory's book and *ONE* for a third time. Then I hid them all.

So I sat down to do some more soul searching. I said, "All right, I'm a homosexual; just what does that really mean?" The first thing it meant was that I knew I had to resign the pastorate of my church. I was sure that the church couldn't come to terms with my homosexuality. No one in it would really understand the feelings that I had. But I also knew that I couldn't change myself. I couldn't fight myself any longer. I didn't think I was sick. I was sure that homosexuality wasn't the disease it was thought to be. And I'd never heard of or met a "cured" homosexual. I'm convinced that there isn't any such thing. You may have a homosexual whose sexual life is expanded to include women, or to have heterosexual experience predominate, but he is essentially a homosexual. Society and the law insist that he is a homosexual right down the line.

Once more I got dressed up to go and state my case. I went over to Compton, California to see my district overseer. I had made an appointment. I walked in, and he greeted me warmly, and wanted to know what seemed so urgent about this visit.

I told him, "Brother, I think I have a problem."

"You better sit down, and tell me what kind of problem you think you have," he replied.

So I sat and said, "Well, I think I'm a homosexual."

For a minute I thought he was dead. He turned as white as a sheet, and seemed as if he was going to fall off his chair, but he pulled himself together and recovered his voice enough to ask, "Tell me something! Have you molested some little boy in Sunday school down there in Santa Ana or somewhere else?"

"No, nothing like that, at all."

So he leaped on that and asked, "Then, what makes you think you're a homosexual?"

I told him, "Well, I read this book, and it tells me that I am." I described the books and the magazine.

He said, "This is a trick of the devil!" That was the attitude that expressed most Pentecostal's correct doctrine. All things thought evil, all sicknesses, all that is thought immoral in any way comes from the devil. We believe in trusting our bodies to the Lord. We try to avoid using medicines. We pray and seek divine healing or divine guidance.

The district overseer said, "We're going to pray about this."

I shrugged, and said, "This'll sound kind of funny, but it doesn't work. I've prayed until I'm blue in the face about this, and God just doesn't seem to understand, or he doesn't answer my prayers about this for some reason."

He looked hard at me, shook his head and said, "We're going to pray again, right here, and right now." So we did. Well, our prayers shook that office. And when we finished praying and got up off our knees, he said, "Now, I want you to go back to Santa Ana, tear up that book, and forget about all of this nonsense. Just forget, as though it's never happened."

"Well, I'll go back to Santa Ana," I said, "but I think you should tell the bishop what I told you." And I left. I looked back, and saw him standing in the doorway, looking rather troubled, and at least slightly bewildered. I got back to Santa Ana all right, but I didn't tear up that book.

I sat down and read that book, and all of them, and all of those magazines over again. And it just refortified everything that I thought about myself. About a month later, the state overseer who is the bishop of our church came to Southern California for an official visit. The district overseer told him what I'd had to say. He just kind of dropped it into the course of the regular business discussions. And the bishop almost had a heart attack. Finally, he recovered, and said, "If he thinks he is a homosexual, there is probably a pretty good chance that he really is! And I want him to resign!"

Well, around Santa Ana, I was beginning to itch a little. And when you itch you've got to scratch. I'd just finished the rereading of my whole new library again, and that really put the lid on it. I picked a nice-looking man out of my congregation; I was sure he was gay. It turned out he also hustled. I just walked up to him and said, "How would you like to stay over and spend the night with me tonight? My wife's back East, and she's been gone quite awhile."

He gave me a long, knowing look and a big smile and said, "Why sure, if you promise not to molest me." And that was all she wrote. I came out. I knew that whatever I lacked, I'd find it only with other men. Only then would my life be totally fulfilled.

Then two things happened in rather quick succession. My wife came home with my boys, and the bishop came to see her. I was delighted to see Gloria and the boys, because I really genuinely loved her, and I adored my sons. We'd just gotten the big welcomes over with when the bishop showed up. I was away at the time. I knew that my wife knew that something was wrong between us, and she probably suspected what it was. I got back home from work that day, and my wife said, "The bishop was just here with the district elder and the overseer, and they all want you to stay here until they get back." She looked at me rather distantly, and added, "They had another minister with them." We both knew that that would constitute a legal board of action, a council, as far as the church is concerned. And they can conduct business pretty fast. She pointed out to me, "I know, Troy, that sets up a council in the church. Now, please, Troy, tell me what's wrong!"

I just looked kind of clumsy, I guess, and said, "I just don't know how to tell you."

"Well, I've been cleaning house, since I got back. And I wonder if it doesn't have something to do with that book you've hidden between the mattresses?"

I leveled with her, gave a steady look, and said, "Yes, it does. I think I'm a homosexual."

"Well, I've known about that in the past. And I read that book, too. You know it said there that a lot of homosexual men are married to women, and yet they make a go of it. Maybe we can stay together and work things out. We can try. You can even have one night out a week with the boys, if you think it'll help."

I just hung on to my feeling of having to do the honest thing. I knew I was hurting her and hurting me. And I knew it was a cruel thing to do to my boys, but I had to let her know that I didn't think it would work out!—that we should really separate. I said, "Come on now, Gloria, you know that wouldn't work. You know me better than that. It just wouldn't work for me. And I know it wouldn't work for you. We have to be really honest with each other about this. It just couldn't work. I don't know how to tell you or anyone else that the only way I feel really complete is with another man. That's it!"

She asked, "What am I going to do? What do you want me to do?"

I could only say, "I don't know. I just don't know what either of us will do—not at this point."

So we were silent for a time, and she said, "Well, I think I want to go back home."

I knew all the pain that that implied for both of us. But I could only say, "All right, if that's the way you feel, then that's what should happen. I can probably tell you more after the church meeting tonight."

Just then the phone rang, and it was the bishop. He said, "We've called all the church members and they'll be at the meeting tonight. All we want from you is to just get up and say that you feel like you failed the Lord and that you're resigning and then you can leave. And they'll never know why you're leaving. And we'll appoint the new minister to take your place right after that."

That night the church members did meet. They were all curious to know why the meeting was called at this time, and what was really up. The bishop got up and addressed them, and said that I had something to say to them. I got up and said, "I'm resigning my pastorate of the church, because I feel that I've failed the Lord." That went off like a bomb. During the stunned silence, before anyone could really ask anything about it, I walked out of the meeting. As I drove off, I could hear the commotion behind me. The congregation backed the bishop into the corner and demanded to know just why. I heard that they wanted to know, and kept insisting upon any logical reason why I would take my family and just walk out on them. Finally, the bishop used the word homosexual. When he did, it just scared the group to death. They shut up fast and never asked another question.

I went home and told Gloria that I was no longer a pastor with a congregation, and we both wept over that. The next three days were pure hell. We packed everything in the parsonage and got ready to leave. We packed up the boxes and things that Gloria would take with her, along with the children. We sold all of our furniture. And we really took a big loss on that. Every time we sold something, and the buyer came and got it, we both cried. In some ways we both knew that it would be a long time before we saw each other again. We knew that we were tearing up five years of our lives together. And we were dissolving our family. My oldest boy, "little Punkin" we called him, kept asking us why we were doing this, why we were moving, and most agonizing, why we were crying.

Finally, it was all done. I packed them up in the car, and took them to the terminal so they could take a bus back to the Midwest and be with her parents. It was a long tearful ride. We both kept saying, "Now, we're not going to cry." But we did. We kept saying, "We don't know why we're doing this, but it'll work out." We knew deep down that it wouldn't, that this was the end. There was to be no more future for us together. I took them into the terminal, and I got the tickets and the luggage all taken care of. It helped hold me together. The bus was called. I kissed both of my boys goodbye and embraced my wife and kissed her goodbye. I asked my wife to watch over the boys closely. And I told my oldest little boy, "Now, you've got to help your mother. Even though you're only three, you've got to help your mother with the little one." That delighted him, and they settled down. I waved goodbye as they pulled out. I went back to my car and got in and just went all to pieces. I cried. I really had an honest to God crying jag breakdown.

And I remember I kept saying over and over again, "Oh, God, why me? Why me?"

Finally, I was able to pull myself together enough to drive back to Santa Ana to the parsonage. I walked in and brought my luggage out to the car. Then I checked the house to see that nothing was left. There wasn't anything. It was as bare and unlived in as though we'd never ever even been there. I knew I'd never be in this position again ever. I swore I wouldn't. And I turned and left. I shut the door behind me, carefully, and locked it. I had closed a chapter in my life that is, even now, painful to recall. I haven't seen my sons since then. But I know I will one day, and they'll know and understand. I'm sure of that.

Chapter Five
The Gay Scene

I felt a great lump inside me. I just didn't know which way to turn. Luckily, a part of my family was living in Los Angeles. My mother had remarried, and lived over in Huntington Park. I went to Mom and told her all that had happened. She told me to move in and stay there for as long as I wanted to. She knew I had to sort things out, and to get over my loss. I mourned for a life I had given up and for my two sons. And I was very unsure of the life I was going into.

It was very hard for me for a time. I looked for work every day. It took me three months to find a job. Preachers who are unemployed are suspect, and finding work, for them, is not at all easy. I know, I went through it.

But I finally got a job selling. And I liked it. I sure needed the money. The job boosted my morale. I had agreed to support my sons, and that took a steady income. I wanted to do that anyway.

New friends of ours in Huntington Park were Marianne Johnston and her three sons. I got to know her very well. She was a really sympathetic person. So were her three sons. I think that basically they were all straight, but one of them was fairly well clued into the gay scene. He almost knew more about it all than I did. And he was only a couple of years out of high school. He told me that he would take me around to places that he had heard about, and that he'd introduce me to people who could show me the scene in Southern California, or at least get me to meet people who could.

Some people think I was licking my wounds, or trying to get it all together. Well, I was. I went around to various gay bars and spots, but cruising really wasn't my scene. Sure, I had one-night stands. I used to go to a couple of gay coffee houses. I really didn't drink at all, so there was no point in my hanging around gay bars. I either scored quickly or just went home and forgot all about it.

Then, too, I was looking for some permanent digs. Buck, my mother's husband, and I got along very well. He was different from most of the men in her life. But he was a really good guy. He understood. And he talked with me about my problem. But I knew that I had to be either on my own or with someone of my own kind.

One night, one of the Johnston boys took me to a gay coffee shop we frequented. That's where I met Willie Smith. Willie was one of my first real friends in the gay community. He still is one of my best friends today. He's a pillar of the church, and our music director. Well, there we were in The Shop on Hollywood Boulevard at Bronson. I think it's now an office building. We walked in and one of the people with Willie Smith sized us up and came over and introduced himself. We all made introductions. Willie was with two youngsters and also his regular roommate. Well, Willie was a very straightforward, shoot-from-the-hip type of gay guy. He worked as a projectionist in various movie theaters. He still does. And he was a right guy. He had two housemates with him. They referred to him as "Mother," and in a way Willie was. He came on strong. He didn't care what anybody said, or thought about him. He was out all the way, and as honest about his sexuality as anyone I've ever met. That's what endeared him to me. He's a big guy, and I wouldn't advise anyone to mess around with him. He could play it straight if he wanted to. But he doesn't want to. He doesn't really camp it up much. He's not nellie. But if he wants to, he can play it any way, and on any level. He could give any queen I've ever met double in spades, as they say.

Willie warned one of his mates to be careful, I looked like a vice cop. But we got along okay. I really wanted to meet gay people in their twenties and thirties. But a lot of the kids hanging around were in their late teens or early twenties. They turned Willie on. And a lot of people in the place knew Willie. Well, I found out that he helped a lot of these young people out. He gave them a place to stay the night, and a meal. His place in Hollywood was like a halfway house or dormitory where young people could crash 'til they found a contact that could help them get started. Sometimes we did the bar scene. Willie was really wising me up to the whole gay scene. From him I learned the language or the lingo, the signals, the grapevine, the whole world of communication that goes on in the subculture of the homosexual community.

Willie was from Arizona. He'd been a member of the Seventh Day Adventist Church. It is a conservative sect with very little ritual. Morally, the sect is very straightlaced. But I think that having Willie know about my background helped cement our friendship. We went a lot of places together, and we did a lot of things together. We were never lovers, only friends. But I could always talk to Willie about anything. I still can. Willie had given up on organized religion. I often talked to him about going back to church. It was so hard for me to try to make any kind of life without it.

This all threw Willie for a loop, because he figured that since I'd been thrown out by my churches, and persecuted for being gay, and the church rejected me for being a homosexual, that it was crazy even to want to go back. But I could see no other way to communicate with God, except through the established churches. I thought again of trying to give up being a homosexual. Willie said, "Well, I don't think you'll ever make it, but if that's your bag, go ahead. But I don't think it bothers the good Lord, so why should it bother you?" Well, that was not only food for thought, it also began the germination of an idea.

One time I felt rather down in the mouth. I had had some bad experiences at work, and I again talked of giving up the gay scene and going back to church. This time Willie really leveled with me. He said, "Oh, now you're not going to run and hide and go through all of that again. You're gay. And you're going to stay gay and you're going to face it. Look at me. I'm gay. I'm a homosexual. And I have to face life, and you have to do the same thing." Well, it was so honest and direct and so sincere that I really thought it over for a long time. Sure, I said my prayers and tried to communicate with God every day. But it was a very lonely way of trying to hack it.

Willie moved out of Hollywood and into Huntington Park. He could get a bigger house if I would share it with him. And I was really glad to do that. It was a ramshackle pink duplex. There was room for Willie, and his family, and me.

Marianne Johnston lived right next door with her three sons. Even though Willie is a chicken queen (one who goes for younger homosexuals), I don't believe he ever made the scene with any of her boys. He was too busy. They were too busy, and Marianne kept a pretty close watch over them. But she knew the score all right. They all did. Well, we all became the best of friends. We confided in her about our troubles and Marianne and the boys confided in us.

We patronized a gay bar in Huntington Park. It was called The Islander. There, it was a case of live and let live. The police never rousted the place. I never heard of anybody getting arrested inside, or even outside. Nobody seemed to care. The police chief kept his force on the beats trying to prevent crimes of violence, burglary, and robbery. That's the way it should be.

Things kind of settled in, and went along fine. Then in the spring of 1965, I got a notice from my local draft board. *Report for induction.* I thought that they must be kidding. I had to support two children. And I was an admitted homosexual. Positive that this would be a breeze, I went down to set the record straight at the local board. I was sure that they were mistaken. So I explained everything to them. I made an appeal. For weeks I fought the battle of the bureaucracy. It was like some disease that flares up just when you think you've got it under control. I'd get a notice to report for a physical. I'd have a physical. I'd have a notice to wait. Finally, in October of 1965, I was inducted. It happened fast. I took my last physical, was sworn in, boarded a bus, was taken to the airport, boarded a waiting plane, and was flown directly to Fort Polk, Louisiana. That's where I did basic training.

First, you lose all privileges, you become almost dehumanized. That's because you have no responsibilities. I was in with a lot of teenagers, so they kind of looked to me. I played it cool. I followed some advice that Willie had given me just before I left. "Keep your mouth shut and your bowels open and *never* volunteer." I passed that on to some of the other boys with whom I was doing the total obstacle course of basic training.

There must be some way to get out of this man's army, I kept telling myself. I asked around. Finally, I went to see the chaplain. It wasn't easy, because they kept us busy at least sixteen hours a day. Training was rough, so we really konked out when we hit the sack. But I explained everything to the chaplain. He listened very sympathetically, and said he would take my case under advisement, and see what he could do.

Time went on, and I kept asking the chaplain what was

going on. It finally dawned on me that he probably was either conducting an independent, private investigation of his own, or he just plain didn't believe me, and was sitting on my case file. I never did find out for sure.

Toward the end of the second week of basic training, I was coming back from sick call. I'd had the inevitable cold that finally knocks you out. I think it's mostly fatigue. Just as I walked into the barracks, the first sergeant called me in. He was a fairly rough customer. He said, "Perry, come in, and sit down. I want to talk to you. Just what the hell did you tell the chaplain when you were down there to see him?"

I just assumed that the chaplain had told him. I looked up and smiled innocently and said, "Oh, I'm a homosexual."

The first sergeant looked blank, jerked himself out of his chair and yelled, "A homosexual? Oh, my God! Cut out the bullshit, Perry! Every day fifteen people come in here and tell me they're queer. Can't you think of something better to get out on? Well, I'll tell you what I'm going to do. I'm going to send you to see a psychiatrist. And, when the report comes back that you're not a queer, I'm going to kick your ass all over this post. Now get out of here!"

I stood up, and said, "Okay, fine with me." So I left.

The appointment was two weeks away. Then it got postponed. Most of basic training was behind me. We were all just about to be graduated, when the first sergeant yelled at me one day, "Perry! I want you to go up and talk to the captain, and tell him about what you told me." Well, I did. I walked in and saluted the captain. Everything was very formal and military. I reported as ordered. The captain returned my salute and told me to sit down. I did.

The captain said, "Are you having any problems?"

"No, sir," I replied.

He relaxed a little, and said, "Well, the first sergeant told me what you had to say to him and to the chaplain. Now, if you do start having any problems, you come in and see the first sergeant. Is that clear?"

And I said, "Well, really sir, he's not my type."

The captain was not amused. He snapped to and said, "Get out of my office!"

I got up, snapped off a salute, did an about-face and left. My mind was made up. I figured that I had done the right thing. I disliked the army. I wanted out. I had told them that I was a homosexual. Whatever happened, the army would be at fault for not acting upon information it already had. That certainly wouldn't be the first time. Actually, I felt rather relieved. So, I graduated and had a short leave of two weeks, and then I was to report to Fort Gordon, Georgia for advanced infantry training.

Gay life in the military establishment? You bet! I was supposed to go to school at Fort Gordon to learn teletype work and cryptography. It was all classified work, and it was fascinating. School work was a snap after basic. And we all had more free time. We cut up and carried on something fierce. There were a lot of gay kids on that post. It was really something else.

The first night I was there, I had been assigned to a top bunk. Well, I checked in and unpacked and decided to log a little sack time. I was just dropping a card back home to tell everyone I'd arrived safe and sound when I heard some music, really wild music. And everybody was quiet because one soldier had started to dance out in the center aisle of the barracks. Wow! What a dancer. He was slim, lithe, and probably the most agile person I'd ever seen outside a circus. Well, this young dancer was so obviously gay that I was really surprised to see him in uniform. He was undoubtedly the nelliest G.I. I'd ever laid eyes on. Well, there was a center post in the barracks, and this young man really worked that post into his dance routine. He was making the dance up as he went along, but I've never seen anything so spontaneously sexy. He hugged that post, and gave it one of the most lewd dance routines anyone could imagine. Well, he went through a whirlwind finish, broke the place up to wild applause, and bowed off. He was standing right close to me.

I gave him a big smile and said, "Hi, my name's Troy. What's yours?"

He grinned back from ear to ear and said, "Hi, my name's Ryd."

We became great friends. He was sort of my sister in the service. We really cut up and carried on something fierce. We exchanged gay jokes. Most of the kids were only seventeen or eighteen. A few were nineteen. I was several years older. My seniority gave me an added status. The younger ones sought me out for advice, and to bring problems to. I could also help them with some of their classwork. We all figured quick ways to beat the system. I had college training, but most of the G.I. classes were taught on about a sixth-grade level. The teachers put me to work helping to grade papers, monitoring classes, and doing things like that just to keep me under control. But it only served to strengthen my position with most of the people in our company. There were always two or three smart ones in the class, and we ganged together to beat the system. It worked like a charm.

On our passes, we went in to town and met more gay people. We really balled the jack. I made some great friends, people I still know and correspond with today.

When school ended at Fort Gordon; we were flown to New York. Some drew other posts, some went on to Europe. I boarded the USN Patch for transfer to Germany. When we walked up the gangplank, every other man had his name taken for KP. That meant that you were permanent KP all the way across. I didn't want any part of that, so I made sure that they couldn't see my name tag. I had a piece of tape that was draped over it. Once on board, I rushed down to the sergeant major's office to see what was up, and what assignments were available. I had heard that they needed a librarian, so I volunteered. The sergeant major asked me if I liked children.

"Oh, I love children," I said.

"Did you ever work with children?"

"Just lots of times. I taught them in Sunday school and Bible classes, camp—you name it."

He smiled. "Real fine. We need someone for the game room, and you're it."

So I was. This consisted of checking in and out the equipment like shuffleboard sets, chess sets, checker games, and children's toys. There were wives and children of servicemen going over. One requirement was a Class A dress uniform at all times. The shift was twelve hours.

During the first three days of the crossing we had real winter storms. Everyone got seasick. The kids would come down and check out stuff, take it to their cabins, and return it later, often totally wrecked. At the end of the trip while in the English Channel, we hit another patch of terrible weather. Everyone was tossed all over the ship.

When we finally docked, the color returned to our faces, we stopped feeling woozy, and our legs stopped being so rubbery. But we marched with all of our gear right onto the trains for our assignments. Mine was at Kaiserslautern in southern Germany. I was posted to the 32nd Army Air Defense Command. They needed four people, and I was the fifth, an extra. What to do? They had to figure out whether I or one other fellow would stay. The other fellow's father had served there and knew the sergeant major. So he got the job. My post was switched to the other side of town to the 94th Artillery Group Headquarters. I thought it might be like going to Outer Mongolia because everyone had looked at me as if it was the end of the world when I got that end of the stick.

That only strengthened my determination to adapt, and make the best of whatever the situation would be. I didn't like the military system. I had learned to use it, and work through and around it. Everyone who adjusts to the military has to figure out his own way of beating the system. Most of the gay kids figure that out first. There were a lot of gay soldiers in my new outfit. There were places in town we went to, and gay bars in Kaiserslautern that got a lot of our patronage. The natives were very friendly.

The sergeant that I worked with was a wildly sexed heterosexual. We were the best of friends. We had to go out and make inspections at various posts in the whole command area. The sergeant and I would get a temporary duty assignment (TDY), and take off. He had a girl in every town; sometimes two or three in any one night. Those German girls just loved him. He loved to be with them, and he seldom spent any money on them. They were always giving him presents and taking him out. Most of them fought over who was going to be his means of support. I should say that I was doing all right on my own, too, but I wasn't as active or bold as the sergeant. My life hadn't been that lurid. He used to amuse me with stories about his career in the military. He'd been in the Canadian Army, the Canadian Air Force, and finally, the United States Army. He was a French Canadian by birth, but an American citizen as a result of his hitch in the U.S. Army. He had been posted to the Congo as an American adviser. He spoke fluent French, which he put to good use teaching the natives there how to use machine guns. At first the natives fired into the air thinking that bullets would come down and strike the enemy on the head and kill him, just as a spear does.

The sergeant taught me a lot of handy German phrases. He knew about me. I knew about him. It was a relaxing live and let live situation—just the way it ought to be. Our relationship was a model for what I'd like to see set up between the homosexual and the heterosexual life styles. We respected and admired each other, and we were close friends.

In Kaiserslautern I started working with a civilian church in the town. It was a Pentecostal church. I thought I could resolve and accommodate both a homosexual and a heterosexual existence. It was worth a try. And I did try. Then I thought, if that doesn't work out, maybe I'll be some kind of celibate and forget all about gender. That didn't work out either.

One thing that had prompted me to seek out God and the church again was the build-up then taking place in Viet Nam. Some of our companies would be reduced in strength to form cadres of new units that were going into special work in Viet Nam. The spectre of going into those jungles, and being named on those mounting casualty lists hung over all of us. It's just as true today that there are no atheists in fox holes, as it was when that slogan came out in the Second World War.

After I attended once, the pastor of that congregation just wouldn't let me not keep attending. I would go, and I would feel the spirit of the Lord. Then I would get accompanying guilt feelings. Why? Well, the memories of the good times I'd had in that gay bar in town would always creep into my mind. I knew from repeated bitter experience just how the church felt. I would be exposed again. And in the army it might mean anything from transfer to discharge, even though they had been told. I was sure they didn't believe it. But I was gradually coming to terms with myself. Finally, I said, "Well, if they find out, they find out. So what." I kept going to church, but I felt so hypocritical about it. It was like going to a Ku Klux Klan meeting, but not believing that blacks, Catholics, and Jews were inferior. There was no easy accommodation. There was none at all. I was drawn to church because going there was the thing to do. Some of my friends went, and I didn't want to be thought different. I felt as I think many suburbanites feel about religion. It has a certain form, but it has only a small place in life. I felt that God had only a small place in what I was doing, especially in my feelings about religion. My former feelings of zeal were largely dormant. I finally dropped church altogether.

My hitch was up; after two long years, I'd made it through to an honorable discharge. I came back to Los Angeles. Willie Smith had taken a smaller place while I was away. He said he couldn't afford the larger one. So now we got back into

Huntington Park, and into the old pink duplex that just coincidentally happened to be vacant again. I went back to my old job and to my old life. Willie and I began to make Miles Avenue in Huntington Park shake. Except for going out on the town, when Willie had a night off, we seldom saw each other. Willie worked nights in the theaters, and I worked days at Sears. Maybe one reason we got along so well together was that we were like ships that passed in the night. We were never together constantly. We were open with each other, and we settled our differences easily. I've never met a more honest person than Willie, especially when it comes to telling you just what's eating him.

One night Willie and I went into Hollywood to a gay place called the Gold Cup. We had just walked through the doorway when there was this wild scream. I thought it would shatter the chandeliers. The person with that loud voice wailed his way over to us and gave Willie a big hello. Obviously they were well acquainted. This tall queen gave me a big hello and said, "Troy Perry, how have you been! God, it's been a long time since I've seen you!"

I said, "My God, George, it has been a long time." My memory was jarred back to before the time I had left for my military service.

George and Willie had grown up in the same town in Arizona. Willie had introduced me to Georgie just before I left for the Army. Georgie confessed that he had had a crush on me, but I had never responded.

We sat down for coffee. We laughed and talked about the possibility of our getting together some time. But I didn't encourage him, just kidded him.

He said, "Troy, when are you and I going to make it together?" He had a twinkle in his eye.

I just nudged him, and said, "Oh, come on now. You know you're not my type."

George said, "No, but I've got somebody who's just your type—just your style."

I said, "You do?" I was always eager to meet someone
new.

George said, "Yes, I do, and I want you to meet him." And
he rotated his shoulder at me.

I said, "Okay, good, where is he at?"

He said, "He'll be along, any minute. He's from Colorado.
'Lonesome Cowboy' type. He's about six feet, with blonde
hair and blue eyes. And when you see him, you'll just keel
over."

Well, Ben showed up. I met him and we clicked. The
friend of Willie's was right. I just keeled over. I fell deeply
and madly in love with him. I don't know why. I couldn't
figure the exact nature of the attraction; it was just there. He
was kind of like the character, "Cowboy" in *The Boys in the
Band.* All the images of sexual attraction that I'd been mull-
ing over in my mind just kind of clicked into place. I not only
keeled over, I fell head over heels in the kind of infatuation
that everyone experiences. I'm sure everyone has had an
experience similar to mine.

We were trying to do some Saturday night bar prowling,
but I'd lost interest. I wanted Ben to be with me. He was. We
had a few beers. We drove back to Huntington Park. On the
way he said he was studying acting. He really wanted to be
an actor. That's why he had hit the Hollywood scene. Back
in Colorado he had started teaching school, but it wasn't for
him. He wanted to make the scene before he got any older.
He was just twenty-one. He said he believed very deeply in
astrology, and that the reason he didn't get along well with
the fellow that had introduced us was because that guy was
a Leo and Ben was a Scorpio.

"You know, Leos and Scorpios clash all the time," he said.
And he was firm about that.

I got to be very defensive because I am a Leo. I assured him
that it wouldn't be any problem if he really set his mind to
it. I thought, wow, he's going to wipe me out before I even
get started.

But that night I took him into the house and showed him

around. I took him upstairs and showed him my bedroom. It was large and had a big bed and a large closet.

He turned to George and Willie and said, "Well, if you don't like me, I'll just stay with Troy." And, with that, he made a grab for me, and I grabbed back.

Well, he spent the night all right. It was like a honeymoon —so much affection. The next day I insisted that he move in.

"Well, I don't know," he said. "I'll have to think it over."

He was living at the Hollywood YMCA, so I took him there the next morning on my way to work. When I dropped him off I made a date for that night to take in a movie. We took in a movie, all right. I can't remember the one we saw on the screen, but we sure had one of our own later that night.

When I took him to the Hollywood Y, I insisted that he move in with me. He said he'd call me later, and, sure enough, that afternoon he called and said, "Okay, I'll move in with you, if you want me to."

That night, he did. I was ecstatic. This was just seventh heaven to me. It was almost unbelievable. I'd never had feelings like this for anyone before in my life. It was my first really open love affair with another man. I'd been out in the gay life for some time, but never anything like this. I hadn't really lived with gay people that much. I knew little about other people's hangups.

But I was determined to help Ben. Most people called him Benny; there was a kind of innocence about him that prompted most people to do so. But his innocent image was often dispelled by his impish, knowing, seductive smile. Two weeks after Benny was with me, his parents called from Colorado offering him a teaching job in a rural school near some town in the Colorado Rockies. He would be teaching eight children in the primary grades. There was a little house nearby that his parents had rented for him and were going to fix up. His salary would be around three hundred dollars per month. There were only two families in that school district, so his parents begged and pleaded with him to come home and take it and be with them. Well, Benny put them off.

The thought that I might lose him got me going right away. The next day I got him a job with me, almost right alongside of me. I had become a division manager in yardage at my job. He went right to work, and turned down the job in Colorado. He did very well, too. He had a winning way. We took our coffee breaks and our lunch hours together. I think we were almost always within sight of each other.

Strangely enough, I didn't realize how totally I wanted to control and dominate him. I wanted him to be almost completely dependent on me. And in many ways he was. Things seemed to run along smoothly. There were things about him, though, that I just couldn't understand. I remember one night he mentioned that he wanted to have a baby. I didn't know what he meant. So I said, "Go ahead, get married to some girl, and change your ways, and have a child, or as many as you want."

Well, he looked at me rather hurt, and said, "No, I want to have your child."

Well, he had said it with such physical urging that I laughed out loud, and he was really upset by that. He was deeply hurt, and I thought that this was just hilarious.

When things calmed down a little, and I had comforted his tears, he said that he was sure he was actually two persons in one body. There was a girl, named Betty, who lived in his body, and there was Benny, the boy. He said that he was sure he'd been torn between these two individuals all of his life.

He said, "Troy, Betty loves you, but Benny hates you." It helped to explain a lot. Betty wanted total dependence. Benny wanted to be independent. Then our frictions started to surface.

We had some violent arguments, actual knock-down, drag-out type quarrels. But I wanted the relationship to work out. I loved him so much. I wanted it to be. I wanted to be with him. And he realized that. He wanted it all to work out, too. He was trying to work out something in his own life. I didn't know what, but I really desperately wanted to help him. I hadn't the least idea how.

One of my biggest stumbling blocks was that I had fallen out of love with God. Benny was my new object of worship and adoration. I idolized him. The sun rose and set in him, in Benny. That was just it. No one could love me the way he did. And I couldn't love anybody else the way I loved him. But I began to have a strange reaction. For the first time in my life I began to have a growing, uneasy sense of failure. That was something I'd never had before in my life. I had always felt that I could do almost anything, that I could accomplish any worthwhile task. Even losing my church congregations, losing my wife and children did *not* make me feel a failure. This experience with Ben began to make me feel so off balance, without aims or goals. I was becoming confused and depressed. I think, finally, the failure of the church to come to any sort of accomodation with homosexuality increased my sense of defeat. I also had to work through the grief that went back to my father's death, to the problems I had later with hidden gay people I contacted, and finally to my own losses of congregation, family and children. I began to feel torn apart in a way I had never actually felt before.

The only thing for me to do was to give church another try. I persuaded Ben to go with me. I felt so good about driving up to that church and going in. I was happy. I felt fulfilled again, just with that anticipation. Benny felt nervous and apprehensive. He didn't really want to go. I hungrily craved that church; it was so in touch with what I had felt was my true calling.

Benny wasn't used to that type of emotional worship service. He'd never been with all of these wildly religious types before. We sang all of the old hymns. I was moved to tears. I felt as if I was getting back home to where I should actually be. But Benny felt trapped. He finally went out and

sat in the car. He said he was never going back in there with
all of those crazy people, and he didn't care if he ever set foot
in a church again. I was so bowled over by this that I was
determined to go back that night alone. I did. But my reaction was totally different. I felt so alone, so dejected. I actually had a feeling of being smothered. I was sure that I
wasn't back where the Lord wanted me to be. I knew that
He wanted me in some kind of church work, but not particularly that church. That was the feeling I had. I became even
more confused. What to do now? That question really
pounded physically inside my skull.

Benny and I almost broke up. I think, in many ways, going
to church was the event that sealed the end for us. It sure
started my mind going a mile a minute. I didn't really go
back to church again with any real feeling that I could make
an accommodation with God until I founded Metropolitan
Community Church. Oh, one time, the next Easter, I helped
a friend of mine, a heterosexual pastor of a Congregational
church in Los Angeles. I helped him twice, once at Easter,
and once again when he had a throat problem. I took care
of everything except the sermon. It seemed like a duty that
I was more walking through than anything else. Aside from
that, I just refused to go back. I prayed a good deal. I asked
for some sign from God. I remember in my prayers I would
ask God where I fit into His plans, what the work was that
He had set out for me. As I waited for God's answer, I felt
that I was kind of wading through life. I had to know what
God wanted me to do. I needed to know that more than
anything else.

Someone told me that the love I had for Benny was all in
my mind. As far as I was concerned, it might have been, but
it was still love.

We thought we could make things work out if we went
on a trip. Willie Smith and I wanted to go with Benny back
to his home in Colorado, and visit his parents. Two things
clouded the issue. Benny didn't want me to go, and I
couldn't get away from work. I'd been promoted again, and

the company couldn't let me go. I was sadly disappointed. The day of departure got closer. As it did, Benny got more withdrawn, more into himself. I knew he worried about the trip. I knew he worried about his parents, and what they might say if they suspected that he was gay. And I was scared that he might feel that everything was over between us. It really was, but I just couldn't accept it. We talked about our feelings for each other. Benny told me that he felt that Betty was losing out in their struggle for me, and that she felt miserable and hurt, but she would be better for it.

The night before they left, Benny said to me, "Well, Troy, it's been great and it's been hell, these past six months with you. But it's all over. I'll move out as soon as I get back."

I could only offer a lame, "Okay."

So, the next morning, I got up, got dressed, and I said to Benny, "I'll see you later." And with that I left. They left sometime in the late afternoon for Colorado, driving straight through. That worried me. I was thinking about accidents, injuries, deaths. I did pray that all would be well.

At work that day I kept thinking, well, if it really is over, let it be really over, really ended. End it. Stop torturing yourself. Stop the agony. So, that night I had something to eat out and didn't even go home and change; I went over to The Island, the gay bar we used to go to in Huntington Park. I walked in, took a table, sat down, and ordered a beer.

I looked the crowd over. I saw the most handsome young man in the place. He was dark complexioned, had a smile on his face a yard wide, and his sexual attraction just wouldn't stop. I knew I'd come there to make a pick up. I knew that I was expecting something that would really end everything with Ben. And it looked like this popular young man, who had everybody swarming around him, was it. People were buying him drinks, or offering to. I saw him go into the rest room, and I did something I'd never done before in my life: I followed him into the rest room expressly to make a pick-up. I knew it was probably the only place I would see him alone. I didn't cruise him, and he didn't cruise me. He was just standing there combing his hair. I said, "Hi, my name's Troy."

He looked me over and said, "Hi, my name's Carlos."

"When am I going to get to see you?"

He gave me a big smile and said, "Well, when do you want to see me?"

"What about tonight, after the bar closes?"

He said, "Fine."

I said, "Okay, I'll pick you up then."

He went on out. I went back and sat down at my table. It was pretty late then, so I just sat down, had one more beer, and toyed with it until the bar closed. When they called out, "Closing time," I went over to Carlos and said, "Let's go!" Just like that.

Carlos said, "I'm all ready."

Well, it startled everyone, especially all those queens that had been fawning over Carlos all evening long.

As we walked out, I heard someone scream, "Look out, he already has a lover!" And that meant me. We went straight to my place. It was as empty and quiet as the grave. I was thankful to have someone with me. As we went upstairs, we stopped and embraced. Then, in my bedroom, we took off our clothes. As we stripped down, I found a letter on my pillow. I knew it was from Ben. I picked it up, and walked over and placed it carefully face down on the dresser. I knew what it would say to me, and I just put it out of my mind. Carlos and I got in bed. He'll never know how much good he did me that night. It was the beginning of a friendship.

Carlos is the young man whose arrest prompted my starting the church. Carlos's case was handled like many others then—like many are handled even today. He pleaded guilty to a lesser charge, disturbing the peace. We all believed, then, that the actual reason for his arrest would not appear on his record. It does. It's an error that we often make. Now, we've learned to fight.

The next morning Carlos left. I dropped him off at the place where he worked. He'd called his people to reassure them that everything was okay. I went on to work. I had Benny's letter with me. I didn't read it until I got ready to go home. I was sitting in the parking lot; I pulled it out and slowly digested its contents. It was a long, rambling letter, and when I finished it, I had such feelings of guilt. I regretted last night's episode with Carlos. I felt that I had committed adultery. I made it home. I broke down again. I went into such an emotional fog that the whole time that Ben was gone now seems like some kind of hazy dream. I was actually physically sick.

Ben and Willie finally came home. Willie plunged back into work. And so did Benny. Benny just totally rejected me. He spoke to me only when he had to. He obviously felt wretched, and so did I. I just couldn't figure out what he wanted. He stayed on at the house, but it was like living in an open grave. He even came and slept with me in the same bed. Yet he treated me as though I were a leper. I didn't know who to talk to. Willie was never around, and wouldn't be for awhile. When he was, I'd hear him say to Ben, "Oh, still hanging in here, huh?" And then there'd be a mumbled reply from Ben.

Three days later I knew that I was near the breaking point. I wouldn't be able to stand any more. We were downstairs alone. I asked Benny if he wanted to go see a movie. He only grunted. I said, "Come on. It's supposed to be good."

He just said, "Nah."

I looked at him and I asked, "Benny, is it really over?"

He looked at me, and smiled, and said, "Yes. It is." And it sounded so final. My world just came tumbling down. I felt so completely lost. I felt like a total failure at everything.

I felt that there was no one I could talk to. I felt shut off from everyone. Nothing seemed worth anything anymore. Nothing had any value. There was no future. Only blackness.

But I wanted to pull myself together. I went into the bathroom and shaved. I put on my after-shave lotion, washed up, and put on my cologne. Then I started crying.

I just couldn't stop. I sat down on the toilet stool. I felt naked, and there was absolutely no one around me. I felt deserted by everyone and by everything that I had ever known. I couldn't remember anything or anyone that had ever meant anything to me. It was hopeless, useless to even try to go on. I couldn't even remember God. I felt as though God did not exist, so why even try to talk to Him. I had lost something I had loved more than anything else in the world. That was the problem, of course. Benny had taken God's place. I had equated him with God. He was "God" in my life, the driving force. Yet, he was human, a very human boy. He had the same parts as I have, or any other man has. I recalled some of the visions I had had in the past.

I could recall always having wondered about Biblical figures like David, like some of the figures from the books in the Bible, and like the people around Christ. My vision of the Angel of Death was like this handsome boy that rejected me. The vision was like the comely youth, John, the Beloved, who laid on the breast of Christ. Christ, who had been betrayed by a kiss from another man, Christ and the men who loved Him. This sweet-faced, youthful vision beckoned me onward. He had left my enemies here on this earth. He had taken my father. He had brought untold hardships to my mother and brothers, and all for what. The images faded. I felt that I had no choices open to me. There was no tomorrow. There was not even the present. I got up and tried to pull myself together. I opened the medicine cabinet. The first thing I saw was the razor blade. I took it. I stared at it. This was the instrument of the Angel of Death. I staggered. I managed to get into the tub; I felt totally numb. I slowly and deliberately, somehow managed to press the blade through the skin and into the flesh of my wrists. The veins popped and yielded up their precious dark fluid. It was thicker than I remembered, and darker, and had an unusual smell that I seemed to detect for the first time. I had physical sensations of numbness growing upon me. I could see the figure of the handsome, sweet youth, the Angel of Death,

beckoning to me. This was the lover I had pursued throughout my life. As the image faded, I drifted off to sleep, even
though I was not at all aware of it.

The dream drifted on; I had a sense of being alive, but of
being asleep, of drifting, of fading, and of being heavier and
heavier. The dream became a troubled nightmare. I wanted
to elude it, but sleep was heavy, and would not leave me.
Somewhere out there I could hear screaming. Scream after
scream filtered through to me, but I could not respond.

Later, I learned that Benny had come into the bathroom,
discovered me in the grisly mess I had made, and just flipped
out. He screamed like a raped banshee and ran next door to
the neighbors. Well, Marianne and a couple of her sons
charged in there and took over. They tied my wrists up with
cloths and rushed me off to the emergency hospital at Huntington Park. But at that hospital, they wouldn't touch me.
By this time, I had come to a bit, and I could talk. One of
the doctors in the emergency room asked me, "How did you
do this?"

I said, "Oh, I was cleaning a window, and must have fallen
through it, and got cut up."

Well, he knew the whole scene. He took a close look at
me, and said, "You'll have to take him to L.A. County General Hospital. The police department down there maintains
a unit, and this has to be reported." So down I went.

By the time I got there I had really gone all to pieces. I
didn't know whether I would live or die. And I was scared.
If ever I went through a complete nervous breakdown, that
must have been it. I was crying uncontrollably. I did feel
terribly human for a change. I must have cried for at least
three hours while waiting for some kind of medical attention. The emergency cases were really lined up.

I was sitting there, crying uncontrollably, when someone
walked in front of me and stood there for a minute. I was
aware of this person, like a shadow before me. This person
reached down and stuck a magazine into my hands and said,
"Here, some of us care!" I looked up dumbly, and stared at

this black woman. It was just like a slap in the face. It snapped me out of my depression, just to hear that someone cared.

My mind started working, just like someone had thrown a switch inside it. I recalled my boyhood as a Southern red-neck cracker brought up to look down on niggers and everybody else. And I couldn't. I had worked with many black people. Once, when I was clerking in a store in Mobile, helping my Mother out, I had called this very friendly black woman ma'am. I called all my elders ma'am. The store manager got on me about that. He told me just to say "yes" or "no," and nothing else.

I said, "Some of these colored ladies are. . .

He interrupted me and said, "There's no such thing as a colored lady. They're 'wimin' or colored folks. You better come over to the meeting we're having Tuesday."

Well, I didn't go to that meeting. It was a Ku Klux Klan meeting. And I got fired. And now, here I was in the emergency waiting room of one of the biggest hospitals in the country, and standing before me was this black lady, who reminded me so much of that other "colored" that I had worked with so long ago. Her head was toward the light. The harsh lights of the corridor gave her a back lighting that was almost halolike. I stared at her. No, she was not the Angel of Life, but in that one moment she had dispelled the Angel of Death. Humanity and humaneness do that.

In a flash I knew that it was over; my fascination with death, with the seductiveness of that angel was over. I had welcomed him as a friend. I would never make that terrible mistake again. I knew now that death, the spectre of death, is an enemy to be feared, fought, and conquered throughout life.

Then the lady left. I never knew her name, but, when I was aware that she had gone, I remembered God. I finally recalled that I had forgotten all about him. There was still God, the Father. It had been so long since I really knew absolutely that He did exist.

I stopped crying. I looked at my soggily bandaged wrists and said, "All right, Lord, I've made some terrible mistakes. You just help me with them." I felt a weight go out of my life. I had been purged. Cleansed. Before I left that hospital I was all right, perfectly all right. I was as calm and cool as I have ever been.

Finally, I was called in for treatment. Everybody charged into the treatment room with me. Benny had recovered enough to come along to help dramatize the situation, and he chose that moment to say, "Oh, you should commit yourself!"

Marianne voiced my feelings, too, when she said, "Now, don't be stupid!"

As one doctor went to work on me, another came along, took one look, and said, "There's nothing wrong with you that a swift kick in the ass won't take care of. You know, don't you, that you're too young for this sort of thing?"

So they sewed me up, and sent me home. I was told to come back in a few days and have the stitches removed.

Fortunately, I had the next day off. Believe me I needed that day to recover. I slept most of the time, and Marianne and the boys came in with hot soup, and milk, and all kinds of goodies. They couldn't get over how fast I seemed to be mending. Benny was gone. The whole thing was really too much for him, and he packed up and left. He said a quiet goodbye, and that he'd see me at work.

He did; the day after my one day off for recovery, I went back to work. No one knew anything about my attempted suicide, but it was just awful. It was the time for our yearly inventory. There was a lot of hard work to be done in the stock room. Since I was the division manager, I had to move goods and material, and to help others who did it. Every time I moved a box, those stitches hurt me. But I gritted my teeth, and I said, "All right, Lord, You teach me. You direct me." So I did make it through the days there. My boss knew something of the problems I had had with Benny. It was hard for me to get over him. There he was. I saw him every day. I saw him come to work. I saw him take off on his breaks. I saw him walk out with others to go to lunch. And every night I saw him leave. The feeling of love was still there. I wanted to tell him how much I had learned, to share with him, but I had learned a lesson. I didn't make a move. I just prayed. I said, "All right, Lord, you know my needs." I studied in earnest. I said, "Lord, this thing about homosexuality. You have to show me, not for my own convenience, nor for my own peace of mind, but really, to let me know, Lord, what does this mean? Teach me, Lord." I studied the Bible, especially the Old Testament. I began to reevaluate everything I had ever learned. There were so many contradictions and so many ideas. I found that you can prove or disprove anything by citing the Bible, and especially, the Old Testament, or St. Paul in the New Testament. But the Lord was guiding and directing me.

I'm sure that He had put me through all of this in order to better equip me for my mission. He was beginning to set in motion the vision I needed for what I had to do, what I had to accomplish in this life. Once set, I found that I could never look back. I haven't.

Chapter Six
God Cares

The pain eased. I knew that I had passed the major crisis of my life. It would never be the same. My whole attitude about God and death and life had shifted. I knew that God cared about me and that He was with me, all the way—wherever that would lead me.

Before, I had always thought that people who talked of suicide or thought about it or tried it were weak. Now I knew that weakness and strength have no part in the whole buildup to suicide. For me it was a closing off of communication, a reaction to loss and rejection, and inability to cope with loneliness and depression. But I had learned, too, that I had to know God. I had to reexperience God. When I had done that, and had grown sure that He was with me always, until the end of my life, I would learn what His mission for me was. I would have that vision. I would be sure.

I relied heavily on Willie, who really took a keen interest

in me. He'd been working the night I had tried to commit suicide. He didn't know anything about it until noon the next day. It shook him. He always said that if he had known, he thought he could have done a lot to head it off. Everybody says that. But I think actually it was something I had to fight through on my own. Strangers might have been able to help me, but no one I knew had picked up on the direction I was headed. I hadn't picked up on it myself. So I didn't know. I was just lucky that I didn't really know how to slash my wrists. It's hard to kill yourself. Fortunately, a lot of people bungle along the way, and live to have productive lives afterwards, but some do go on and on until they perfect their technique and succeed. Each attempt is a rehearsal.

The next-door neighbors were of great help. Marianne and her sons were so eager to help me. They kept a close watch on me. Truly they were the good Samaritans that we have often dreamed of meeting. They understood the problem I had had in trying to adjust from the one-night stand to a real, ongoing love relationship with Benny. I never thought I would see the day when my emotions held such sway over me. I think they were fascinated by my reactions to all of this, too.

A lot of times after I got home, or on my day off, when I got up and got with it, I'd drop in on Marianne for a cup of coffee, and we'd really have some good old-fashioned talk fests. Not just jawboning. She'd really tell me what she thought and ask a lot of questions. So would I. These were real give and take sessions. Marianne was such a genuine, earthy person. She was one of the most understanding people I've ever met, under any circumstances. One of her great friends was a black woman who was a minister. I knew Marianne well enough to know that she didn't gossip.

I finally met her minister friend. She was small and direct, and her name was Vera Hockset. She was truly amazing. She believed in guides; that meant that each person had a guide that helped him through life. She could actually see a person's guide, or so she said. With me that kind of stuff was really a big laugh. I think it is with most people. I was sure it was a lot of crap.

This particular Sunday afternoon, I was next door. Willie was working. All was quiet. And I met Vera. She asked how everything was going with me. And I said, "Oh, I'm just fine."

She looked at me directly and said, "Well, you're not really."

Well, that shook me up a little. I figured that Marianne had really been talking to Vera, but as I see it now, I am convinced she didn't. Marianne just isn't that type.

I talked with Vera. Vera stopped me with one line. She said, "I see your guide." I couldn't figure out what she meant. So she described exactly what she meant. Her sincerity moved me and touched my heart somehow.

She assured me that my guide manifested himself. "He's an Indian," she told me, "and he wears a clerical collar." I must have reacted, but I was sure that Marianne must have told her my story. Vera went on, "Do you have some relative that was a minister? A deceased relative? You have an Indian in your background."

I do, of course. I am part Cherokee Indian on my father's side of the family. I thought she could probably tell this from my high cheek bones. I thought she was able to detect that, or possibly she was an expert at reading personality traits or maybe just plain guessing.

But I told her, "Yes, I had a great-uncle who is deceased, and he was a Pentecostal minister."

Vera went on to say, "You're a minister. You always have been, and it won't be long before you will be pastoring a church."

I just laughed. I was wiped out by that one. I said, "No, I'll never pastor a church."

She looked sternly at me and said, "Oh, yes you will. God has a ministry for you."

That stunned me. All my life I'd always been told that by people who really knew me. And here was a total stranger telling me the same thing. My Auntie Bea used to say the same thing over and over. Now the statement started my thoughts running wild. In all of my Pentecostal experience, I was used to seeing the Holy Spirit—the Spirit of the Lord —move! I knew of the gift of prophecy. Auntie Bea had had the gift of tongues, and the ability to pray for people and see them healed. I remembered that Auntie Bea had one time said, "The Lord has a ministry for you. A great ministry, but it won't be in the church you're in." At that time it almost broke my heart. Now I began to think seriously about that jarring memory, that recollection called up out of the past. I had thought that those churches of which I was a member during my teens were everything I would ever want or need. They were holy and good. I couldn't see anything else, not down in Alabama or Georgia or Florida or even the Midwest. I was trying to think this through, along with the problem of homosexuality. And now these bombshells came from Vera.

I smiled at Vera and said, "It'll never happen." But she topped my smile with one of her own that came from her own basic understanding and warmth. She started to tell me many things about myself, about me and Benny, about how I felt and thought about a lot of things. She told me more than Marianne could possibly have known about me. It really rocked me, and I knew that this was no ordinary woman. She had powers of insight that must have come from God.

This was only another step along the way to my coming to terms with God, to accepting his wider and greater understanding. I prayed a great deal. And the Lord began to deal with me. Things became easier. My attitudes shifted. I felt that my own personal demons that had goaded me on for years had confused me about death. They had tricked me into feeling that death was a friend. I knew that my personal demons were associated with sin. They blocked my own vision of humanity's need, but now as God dealt with me, these personal demons became impotent and powerless.

They were vanquished. Finally with God's help and understanding, I became convinced that He was moving me to a mission, that a vision of that mission would be revealed to me. When it came, I would never look back; I would never have to. My journey would be forward. My course would be clear. I would know my work. It would be hard, but I would spend my life at it.

I prayed. I envisioned God as a father, a kind of image. I could feel His presence. He was not a man, but like a man. He was of this earth, yet not of it. He was an abstract being that I felt was with me. He was the source of power, authority, warmth and understanding. God was the force of good, of energy, of creative positive happenings.

I had time to reflect again on my attempted suicide. I felt that I had faced death, come face to face with it. I found that death wasn't the answer to anything. It is not through dying that we obtain salvation, it is through living and bettering the human condition for all. That is our fight; through faith we can arm ourselves for our crusade. I'm convinced that we must all walk through the Valley of the Shadow of Death, and yet fear no evil—that means no fear of death. And that walk through the valley means a work tour. Our work is one of struggle to free our souls from bigotry, from prejudice, from the dehumanizing forces that attack us. My work is only a small part of that. I know that the God I worship is color-blind. He understands all tongues, all thoughts, all feelings and deeds. It was God the Creator who set in motion all that propels us.

You see, sometimes I think that in my Southern background, I felt that God must surely carry a shotgun. Otherwise why the rigid attitudes that never yielded on such high points of bigotry as color of a person's skin, race, national origin, sexual orientation, life style, religious beliefs, political affiliation, and all the rest. It took my acceptance of my own homosexuality for me to realize that all the barriers of prejudice must come down, not only in my area of life style, but in all areas of intolerance.

After my suicide attempt, I would hit the gay spots once in awhile. Usually I went with Willie on his night off. I ran into Carlos again several times. With us, whatever happened, happened. Sometimes it was a sexual embrace, sometimes it was just having a beer, going for a swim at the beach, or whatever we felt like doing. And we hit the bars. We used to talk about our basic beliefs, but Carlos would never even let me make any mention of religious beliefs. He had mentioned that he had belonged to a church, but, he agreed with Willie Smith: for him it was not the answer.

Then Carlos got busted. For what? Well, just for buying a beer in a gay bar. He had done absolutely nothing else. He was there with me, and with a couple of friends of ours. One of the other fellows with us was also taken in. I mentioned in my introduction to this book how shaken we all were by this experience. It was so unjust. It was just another example of man's inhumanity to man. Then, when his cup of bitterness spilled over, he said, "God doesn't care!" When I recovered from that cold, hard statement I knew I had to act. I knew my course. With each passing day I drew closer to founding a church that would reach into the souls of the homosexual community. My mind was made up.

I used to have to fight to keep it from occupying all of my thoughts while I was at work. I knew that the mission was coming into focus. God wanted me to start a new church that would reach into the gay community, but that would include anyone and everyone who believed in the true spirit of God's love, peace, and forgiveness. My learning experience speeded up. The Lord was really getting me ready. I knew that the word, church, would be in the title. In my free time, I used to try to decide what the rest of the title would be, and just what kind of church did God really want me to found. I would sit in that little office in back of the yardage department and pray and think. I would say, "What about that God?" I knew He wanted a church where He could move. I think that's why church was always in the title. Then I would ask the Lord if it was to be really an outreach into the gay community. So the word, community, got into the title. The more I thought about it, the more I liked it. Community meant a feeling of comradeship, a small area, a place where you knew everybody. So, it would be a community church. We would also serve a large community; we would serve the whole Los Angeles area. Los Angeles is a large urban area, so the word, metropolitan, finally came to mind, and it stuck.

Then I had to worry about how I was going to reach the gay community. There's always the grapevine, but church services and religion aren't usually part of that. The grapevine is for gossip and action mostly.

But, I was a happy individual. Willie Smith saw me walking around the house humming, smiling, and full of energy. He nailed me about it one day. He said, "I know you don't have a new lover, because you'd have him under foot. But what's eating on you?"

So, I leveled with him. I said, "Well, Willie, I'm sure that God wants me to start a new church."

Willie just collapsed and said, "Oh, my God, I thought you were all over all that silliness."

I said, "Wait a minute, Willie. This is a church *for us,* it *will serve the homosexuals,* the gay community."

Well, Willie thought that was crazy. He said, "You mean you really are serious about this religious stuff?"

I assured him that I was. I said, "I know, Willie, that it's the thing to do. I've got to try it and see if I can't bring a message, God's message, to all the gay people."

What Willie wanted to know was this: "How're you going to organize a bunch of queens, and get them to follow any religion, or any person, or do anything together. You know how bitchy they are. They always act individually. Nobody has ever organized the gay community into anything and accomplished anything. It's as ridiculous as trying to get a bunch of crazies in the funny farm to act as a team."

I told Willie I would go ahead anyway. He wanted to

know where and when. I said, "Just as soon as I can get rolling. And we'll do it right here."

Willie was horrified. He said, "You've got to be kidding. I'm already too much for Huntington Park. And you're going to have all those faggots from Hollywood down here running in and out of our house to attend church service? The neighborhood just can't take the strain!"

I said, "All right, Willie, relax. I'm going to do it!"

He just looked at me again, and said, "Okay. If you're going to do it, go ahead. But don't be too disappointed if it doesn't happen. Helping queens get religion isn't anybody's bag. But if it does work, count me in."

Then I asked Lee Glaze down at The Patch about it. Lee thought it would be just great. I asked him what he thought was the best way to reach the gay community. He thought it over.

While he was thinking, I said, "I'm going to advertise it in *The Advocate,* I guess. What do you think about it?"

He said, "That's a great idea. As a matter of fact, it happens that the editor of *The Advocate* and his lover are here in The Patch tonight. Would you like to meet them?"

I was eager to, so I went into Lee's side office near the bar. He brought in Dick and Bill, and made the introductions. We started talking, and I explained my plans. They looked at me as if I was a little weird. They were skeptical about what I was trying to do. Was this some kind of business venture? Was I trying to capitalize on gay people? Just what was I up to? They got on a long discussion on what they thought about people who cashed in on, and often took, the gay community for money with nothing in return. They made it clear that they hated exploitation. They weren't sure that they wanted to sell me any advertising at all. So I really gave them my pitch. When we finished, they not only took the ad, they gave me a good rate on it. They also told me that they might, just might, even attend a service at Metropolitan Community Church (MCC), if it ever got started.

The Advocate was published only once a month. I would

advertise in the October issue which would hit the street the last week of September. So, I set the date for my first service. It was October 6, 1968. I had about two weeks then between the ad and the first encounter.

Just about ten days before the first service, my mother came down to see me. She and her husband were separating, and she was going to go back home to Florida for a vacation. She knew of my suicide attempt, of course, and she kept much closer contact with me. I visited her as frequently as I could.

Again, I'm going to have her tell, in her own words something of the way she saw it.

"I couldn't feel a lot of things back then, when Troy was going through all of this. In our background, everything was a sin. And it surely took a lot of thinking and praying to really realize that many of the old strict ways we were raised with just aren't what it's all about. The real sin is hate and being inhuman to each other. That's how we all sin against the homosexuals. I'm glad that I've been able to discard that attitude in my life.

"I remember that after Troy got out of the army, and came back to Los Angeles, he really was kind of lost. He didn't have his wife or his sons. And he had 'come out,' as they say in the gay world. He lived with us for a time in Los Angeles, and then he moved to Huntington Park. But he was troubled, and it was a trouble that was deep inside him. It wasn't us, nor any of the rest of the family. We knew all about him, and we accepted him and loved him. Whatever he was and whatever he wanted to be was just fine with us. And we all stood with him, stood by him.

"One day I visited with Troy at his home in Huntington Park. He seemed kind of distracted, like he was about to explode. I was afraid that he was losing interest in his faith, in any kind of church or religion. And we were talking. I said to him, 'Troy, have you ever thought about starting a church?' Well, that stunned him. I guess I must have really read his mind. And I wasn't as used to the homosexual life then as I am now. I couldn't see into it. But we were talking, and he told me that what was eating at his heart was that a friend of his had been arrested—busted as they call it—on some kind of homosexual charge or other. And he told how much that boy needed help. And I said to him, 'Well, haven't you ever thought about starting a church for homosexuals?' Well, a change came over him, and he looked at me and that was it. He said that that was just what he was going to do. He looked so fierce and intent. He said that it had been uppermost in his mind for several weeks, but especially the last few days.

"We discussed it a bit more, then I went away; I went back and visited with my family for a time in Florida."

I began to share my dream for the church with the gay guys and gals I met. They almost all had the same reaction that Willie Smith had had. Some told me to forget it, adding that most gays had made their peace with themselves, and that peace didn't include religion. I knew, then, how hard the job would be. We had gone through generations, even centuries, of that awful conviction that if you were a homosexual you could not be a child of God; you could not be a Christian. I was really shoveling sand against the tide to get started.

That first Sunday church service finally arrived. I stood nervously watching the door, worried to death. I had cleaned out the living room, set up some chairs, used the coffee table for an altar. I had borrowed a robe from the Congregationalist minister that I had helped out previously. He insisted that I had to preach in a robe for that first service. I had borrowed some trays from some very close friends, Steve and his lover, Lynn. These were for communion. I set up everything, and stood in the kitchen. Our house was one of those "shotgun" looking houses. From the front door, you could see all the way back. You could see right through to the back room. I could stand in the kitchen and look all the way down the hallway to the front door. I paced nervously around in my borrowed robe and clutched the Bible and

thumbed through it and riffled the pages. Then, people began to gather. Willie let them in. He greeted them, and saw
that they sat down. One friend of ours brought his straight
brother and the brother's girl friend. Other people showed.
Most had heard about it, but, finally, three people showed
up who had read the ad in *The Advocate.*

There were twelve in the living room, and I walked out,
and asked everyone to stand up, and I said, "We'll go before
the Lord in prayer." We joined hands and prayed. Then I
said, "We'll sing some hymns." I invited everyone to turn
to a page in the book. We'd borrowed the hymnals from the
Congregationalist church where I had been a guest preacher
the previous Easter.

No one knew what to expect. Everyone was as scared as
I was. They all waited around for me to lead the singing and
sing out. Well, I did. My mother always used to say, "My
boys don't sing too well, but they sure sing loud." And that
was never truer.

As we sang, I recalled Marianne Johnston's reaction to the
church. She thought it was a lovely idea, but she said,
"You'll be raided during your first service."

I laughed and said, "Well, I wish the police would come
in. It wouldn't bother me at all."

We sang several hymns. They sounded a little thin and
sour, but the spirit was what counted. We didn't have a
piano or any kind of accompaniment. It seems strange now,
Willie Smith was there, but he wasn't sure he wanted to be
a part of it. He still didn't know just what to think.

I recall I had assured Willie just before we started that God
was in this. I said, "I know now that I'm going to be in God's
perfect will. Not his permissive will as I was in my past life."
When we sang the second hymn, I recalled this talk with
Willie. I reached that part of the service where I had to get
down to cases. We again prayed.

Then I relaxed. I introduced myself. I told about where I
was born, my age, my name, my marriage, my sons, my
religious background, where I went to high school and col-

lege. I talked about the churches I had pastored in Florida, Illinois, and California. I said that one in Santa Ana had been the last I pastored in 1963, and here we were now, after my army hitch. I told them that I was a division manager with one of the largest retailers in Los Angeles, and that I would continue as such until the church was large enough to support a full-time minister. Even then, I was sure that that time would come. Then I introduced the church. I said the church was organized to serve the religious and spiritual and social needs of the homosexual community of greater Los Angeles, but I expected it to grow to reach homosexuals wherever they might be. I made it clear that we were not a gay church; we were a Christian church, and I said that in my first sermon. I also told them that we would be a general Protestant church to be all-inclusive. Then I prayed again. And I then went into my Biblical message.

My sermon was entitled, "Be True To You." It was actually inspired by Polonius's advice to his son, Laertes, when the young man was about to leave. It's early in Shakespeare's play, *Hamlet,* and it's from those lines that go: "This above all: To thine own self be true, And it must follow, as the night the day, Thou canst not then be false to any man."

I then moved from Shakespeare to the story of Job, to the Book of Job, chapter 19, verses 1-26, and I read them aloud.

> Then Job answered and said, How long will ye vex my soul, and break me in pieces with words? These ten times have ye reproached me: ye are not ashamed *that* ye make yourselves strange to me. And be it indeed *that* I have erred, mine error remaineth with myself. If indeed ye will magnify *yourselves* against me, and plead against me my reproach: Know now that God hath overthrown me, and hath compassed me with his net. Behold, I cry out of wrong, but I am not heard: I cry aloud, but *there is* no judgment. He hath fenced up my way that I cannot pass, and he hath set darkness in my

paths. He hath stripped me of my glory, and taken the crown *from* my head. He hath destroyed me on every side, and I am gone: and mine hope hath he removed like a tree. He hath also kindled his wrath against me, and he counteth me unto him as *one of* his enemies. His troops come together, and raise up their way against me, and encamp round about my tabernacle. He hath put my brethren far from me, and mine acquaintance are verily estranged from me. My kinsfolk have failed, and my familiar friends have forgotten me. They that dwell in mine house, and my maids, count me for a stranger: I am an alien in their sight. I called my servant, and he gave *me* no answer: I entreated him with my mouth. My breath is strange to my wife, though I entreated for the children's *sake* of mine own body. Yea, young children despised me; I arose, and they spake against me. All my inward friends abhorred me: and they whom I loved are turned against me. My bone cleaveth to my skin and to my flesh, and I am escaped with the skin of my teeth. Have pity upon me, have pity upon me, O ye my friends; for the hand of God hath touched me. Why do ye persecute me as God, and are not satisfied with my flesh? Oh that my words were now written! Oh that they were printed in a book! That they were graven with an iron pen and lead in the rock forever! For I know *that* my Redeemer liveth, and *that* he shall stand at the latter *day* upon the earth: And *though* after my skin *worms* destroy this *body,* yet in my flesh shall I see God.

Job had learned to be true to himself. He never wavered once he made up his mind, and knew that he was called of God. His friends came and told him that he must have sinned for some reason or he wouldn't be visited by all these bad nasty things that plagued him. He lost his family. Everything terrible happened to him. But Job's remark to them was, "Though God slay me, yet I'll trust Him. I'll come forth

as pure as gold." Even going through the refiner's fire, he
knew that he would make it. And I knew that we at Metropolitan Community Church could do that too. Also, I
preached about David and Goliath. David said that the same
God that protected him when he had to do battle once with
a bear, and once with a lion would protect him again. Even
when things look awfully bad to us in the gay community,
God can help. And we can win, even though it looks like
everything is stacked against us. So, I said, "Be true to you.
Believe in yourself, and believe in God. You have to believe
in yourself as a human being first, and then God is able to
help you. You are not just an individual in circumstances,
but you always are the created being of God." And then I
told the story of J. C. Penney, the gentleman who developed
one of the biggest retail chains in the world. I talked of his
trust, his belief in the Golden Rule and what that did for
him. He was true to himself, no matter how he was ridi-
culed. Some laughed at his mixing his belief in his version
of the Christian principles with retailing. But he stuck to it
and developed the second biggest retail chain in the country.

I pointed out that we must be humble human beings first,
homosexuals second. We must love and build, free ourselves, and free others from their feelings against us. I closed
my sermon with a quote from The Epistle of St. Paul, the
Apostle to the Philippians, fourth chapter, thirteenth verse,
which says, "I can do all things through Christ, which
strengtheneth me."

After I finished preaching, I closed my Bible, and I knew
that God was in the place. I prayed again, and when I looked
up, and said, "We're going to have open communion," there
wasn't a dry eye in the place. Everybody in that small living
room was weeping silently. We all felt that we were a part
of something great. God was fixing to move. We were to see
His handiwork, and that would be unbelievable.

Marianne Johnston had given me a glass plate to serve the
communion bread from. The bread had been supplied by my
Congregationalist minister friend. It was the same type of

wafer that is used in Catholic and other services. Two friends had given me a cup for the wine. It was not really a chalice; it was a "Jefferson Cup." They gave it to me personally as a souvenir of the occasion. I still have it, and I prize it very highly.

I offered communion. Only three came forward to take the bread and wine, but they were weeping. And then I served communion to myself. We dismissed with a prayer of benediction. Then I invited everyone to stay for coffee and cake. We gathered and we just couldn't quit crying. We all sat around and said we had felt the spirit of the Lord. One young man came up to me, and said, "Oh, Troy, God was here this morning! I haven't been in a church in eight years. And even when I left the church, the one I'd been in, I never felt anything like I felt here this morning, in this living room."

When that service was finally over, Willie Smith said that he had really been moved by it. He insisted that he didn't know yet about whether the church would actually take a hold and grow. I said, "Willie, only God knows the answer to that."

But Willie said, "It just might, and I want you to know I'm with you all the way, one hundred percent. And I'll do anything I can to make it work." And he has. He started right then. For the next Sunday, he scrounged up a phonograph and records of some religious music so that we could all sing to it. Aside from being an ace projectionist, Willie is also a singer, and music director. He made that his job. He still has it. And it grows all the time.

The next Sunday we were fourteen instead of thirteen. I got up and looked around and said, "If you love the Lord this morning would you say amen!" They all shouted amen back to me. It's been that way, too, since then. I also praised the Lord because we were growing.

The next Sunday we had sixteen, and I got up and said, "Well, look at this. Thank you Jesus, we're on the move!" But, the fourth Sunday, we had only nine, and I almost died.

But here again, God had prepared me. He gave me a sermon entitled, "Despise Not The Day Of Small Things." And God gave me that sermon for Troy Perry, not for anyone there.

Lee, a friend from my army days, and now one of the regulars, said, "That morning, when you looked out in the group, and saw that it had shrunk, I could tell that you were upset. You got up and you preached, and you preached as though you meant it. I could tell you really meant it."

I said, "Well, that sermon God gave me for me." The next Sunday we had twenty-two in attendance. We'd jumped back up, and we've never dropped since.

As we started to grow and attract people from all kinds of different backgrounds, I knew that we would have to get down to cases about settling problems of organization, administration, doctrine and the church services. They had to be settled soon, so that everyone would be able to know and rely on the church, to really be a part of its body, of its identity.

I knew that I was not starting another Pentecostal church. I was starting a church that would be truly ecumenical. I had asked the religous backgrounds of those first twelve. They were Catholic, Episcopal, and various Protestant sects. I fervently sought to serve a really broad spectrum of our population. It would have to be a church that most could understandably and easily identify with, and accept it as not being unusual or odd. It seemed to me that it should be traditional, almost like those they attended in childhood, or not too different from that. It wouldn't work if we tried to update it like some cults where Christ came out of a flying saucer. It had to be completely honest. I knew that I couldn't play games. My sermons would have to do as they always had done, relate to the Scriptures and to God. This, I knew, would be the hard part. I am not an intellectual. I have never claimed to be the type of speaker that required the listeners to bring a dictionary to each session. I always regarded myself as a preacher, not as a teacher. Now, I knew that I must be both, especially for those who came to church either for the first time or after years of having no contact with God or established religion. But I also had to reestablish old links with God, but do it in a new way that would be meaningful in our community.

Although I became the pastor and founder, I don't really feel like a pastor, at least not in the sense I'm used to thinking of pastoring. A pastor has all the time in the world to devote to his congregation. He knows all of them on a first-name basis. I used to be that way, but it wasn't long before we'd grown so much that it was impossible. I am an exhorter, a preacher from the pulpit, an evangelist.

At the start I wanted everyone to relate to me as their pastor. Some had trouble doing this because I wasn't wearing a Roman collar, or wearing robes. I talked to those from the more informal sects about this, and they said, "Well, it's not going to bother us. You're still going to be Troy, and no matter what you wear, that's not going to change your preaching." Some said, "As long as it doesn't change your preaching style, or your message, we're for it." So I went out and bought full pulpit attire to help some of my flock relate better. It did help, and it's never hurt anybody. The important thing is that they feel the spirit of the Lord. What I wear doesn't stop them.

We kept our ad running in *The Advocate.* And we also got some great news coverage from that paper. We were news in the gay community. Most regular newspapers, especially the religious columns, ignored us. They felt that if they just ignored us, we weren't there. People kept coming, and we kept growing. My house was bursting at the seams. We were looking for another place to hold services. We needed help on all fronts. I needed other theological minds to help me really finalize the way it was all developing.

One day someone called the house early in the morning. I was away at work, but Willie was home. He was trying to sleep late. As a projectionist he worked late, and at this time, he'd had a particularly long-running film. Willie finally answered the phone. The person asked to speak to Reverend

Perry. Willie said he thought it was a friend of mine, so he said, "Well, you've missed him. He's already at work." The voice showed some surprise and asked where I could be reached. Willie said, "Oh, you know, over at Sears on the corner of Slauson and Vermont."

His caller was delighted, and politely said, "Oh, okay, thank you." And that ended that call.

We were all a little supersensitive because the vice squads were really cracking down all over Los Angeles County. So, when this pleasant young man with bright blue eyes, short wavy hair and a rather stocky build showed up and asked me at work if I was Reverend Perry, I knew he wasn't a customer. I said, "That's right." He said he'd like to talk to me, that if it was all right with me, he would follow me back to Huntington Park, where I lived, and we could have a talk. I asked him to wait outside. It was almost quitting time. I would check out and join him for a cup of coffee. He agreed. So I checked out, got my coat, went right to the phone and called the house. I got hold of Willie, and asked if he'd sent anyone.

He said, "Yeah, someone called when I was asleep, and I told him where to reach you. Who is it?"

I really laid Willie out. I said, "That's what I'm asking you. You tell me. He could be a policeman, I don't know anything about him."

Willie said, "Well, don't get too hot and lose your cool 'til you find out who he is."

I said I was taking him for a cup of coffee.

Willie said, "Good, if you come home singing, 'You're The Cream In My Coffee,' I'll know it was a good trick." We hung up, with me still irritated.

I met this chap, and we hurried into the nearby coffee shop, sat down and ordered. We were alone over in a corner, as he had suggested. The coffee came, and I said, "What's on your mind?"

He said, "I've read about you and the church you wish to

start in *The Advocate.* And I'm interested to know why it is that you wish to start such a church."

I looked at him, and I realized that he was really serious. I said, "Well, surely you must know I'm a homosexual."

If I had tossed a bucket of cold water over him, it wouldn't have shocked him any more. He turned as white as a sheet, and said, "You certainly seem like an honest individual."

I said, "I've got to be. For me there is no other choice." I looked at him carefully, and asked, "Are you a homosexual?"

Well, that really rocked him too. But he made a very good recovery, faced up to the issue squarely, and said, "Yes, I am."

"Now that we've got that out of the way, what's really on your mind?"

"You see, I'm a minister, also. I teach at a Christian college in this area, where I am a dean. But it struck me that what you're doing is a needed step in a new direction. And I am interested in participating." Then he reassured me by showing me his identification. Well, I knew that he would be a great help. We had a long conversation, and that's how my first ministerial recruit came in. There have been many others. But the Reverend Richard Ploen was the first. One reason I was so glad to have him along was because of his education, and because of his work as a missionary. I knew that he would be invaluable in helping to set up an educational program. Many who came had been away from church for a long time. Among the youngsters, some had never been to church. We needed a really intensive ongoing program in Christian education. Richard Ploen dug right in. His background intrigued a good many. He had been a missionary in Omdurman, Sudan, Africa. Among his many skills is the ability to use the sign language of the deaf mute. He taught that in MCC, and set up a section where other deaf mutes convey the entire sermon in sign language. Now others do that work, and teach those courses. Richard has a Master of Divinity degree from Pittsburgh Theological Seminary, and a Master of Christian Education from the Presbyterian School of Christian Education. He is a tireless scholar, and certainly a solid pillar of Christianity.

He helped with music and lead in the prayers. Willie couldn't make it to church every Sunday because he worked, so Richard would tape music for us from the music library at the college where he taught. He helped with all of the service, and especially in formalizing it as it now stands.

His research efforts were most helpful in gleaning what we needed from other denominations' ceremonies. We had little trouble with doctrine. It was a church of doing: do love your God, do stand tall, do walk proud, do love your neighbor as yourself. These were the kinds of things that we wanted to state positively. Because of the large numbers of Catholic, Episcopal, and Lutheran people in our congregation, we relied rather heavily on those rituals.

We decided upon such standard procedures as the one for communion. It would always be an open communion. We would always state that it was. We would extend an invitation for all to come to the Lord's table. We would prepare ourselves by an open act of confession. We would ask for absolution, and it would be granted. We would then participate in the act of supping at the Lord's table, by taking bread dipped in wine. Ministers offer communion, aided by deacons. Finally, when the congregation was cared for, they all in turn took communion.

We utilized the books of worship from the Espiscopal, Presbyterian and Lutheran churches as well as those that members of the congregation wanted considered. We experimented and we accommodated. It may sound like a hodgepodge, but what emerged was a straight line of well organized ritual that allows for improvisation or change should any occasion within the church warrant it. We had some experimental services. Every first Sunday of the month, we took in new members and performed baptisms.

But it is not the mechanics of worship that we were concerned with. It was the substance of the act of worship that was the core of our service. We did have diversity. We needed that. Ours was a working church, an active, growing church. We knew that the worship of God comes from the heart. So we were always free to move and grow. That's the way it has always been. We felt that the diversity and the freedom and the real sincerity of worship would bring us together in unity. It has. We now have a magazine called *In Unity*. When we finally obtained our charter, it was as The Universal Fellowship of Metropolitan Community Churches. In that organization we establish missions and new congregations, and our whole program of social, economic and political action.

We were about ten weeks old when we really had to move to accommodate the crowds. We had three dozen every Sunday, so we made up a delegation and we went to a group in Huntington Park that we thought had the room to accommodate us. It had to be a place we could afford that would have room for us to expand and to grow.

That's what we really needed. We were reaching out into the gay community. We were in our infancy, but we were thriving. Nothing could stop us. We all felt the thrill of discovery, and the occasional clumsiness of growing pains. We knew that we stood on the threshold of great things. God was leading us, and He was moving. We had to do His bidding.

Chapter Seven
Our Militant Stand

People came out of the shadows, out of the closets, out of the half world. They were drawn to the Metropolitan Community Church. For what? Some were curious. Some were incredulous. We were new. We were a novelty. We were an item in the gay world. We were ignored in the straight world. But not everyone in the straight world pretended we were not there. Sociologists, professional people, teachers, professors, psychologists and the enlightened came. They made a great and lasting contribution.

Many who made selfless and really generous contributions of time, effort, money and real hard work must still remain anonymous because the great swamp of prejudice that could engulf and destroy them is still around us. Nevertheless, all gained strength and courage as we united and took our position, a position of pride and equality.

One of my best friends and colleagues falls into the category I have just mentioned. I'll call him Lou Lindsey. He and his lover Lee came to church when we were still only one dozen strong. Lou was on our first board of directors, and later he helped found the Universal Fellowship of Metropolitan Community Churches. Lee was our first social director. He planned a really ambitious program for all of us, and it was really successful. We had parties, dances and festivals, each more swinging than the last. Lou was a driving force at the start. He still is. He has a keen mind in anticipating our needs, and how to meet them.

Another person to come forward was Professor Barry Dank, a professor in sociology at California State College, Long Beach. Although he is a heterosexual, he has worked long and hard to give direction to the social arm of our church. He has trained people to handle crisis situations, and has helped us examine and then reexamine the gay life style. Courageously, he taught the first college course on homosexuality. He has an active research program going on the gay life. He once told me that when I said something was going to happen, it did, but that he hasn't figured out why. I reassured him, "God moved! I just work for Him."

Later, Dr. Martin Field of the University of California at Los Angeles Neuropsychiatric Institute gave a course on crisis intervention and counseling, and has an ongoing counseling program with us.

Our church provided a feeling of freedom to worship, to walk with God. We know that we were on His side because He loved us, too. We excluded no one. We welcomed everyone. We still do. Heterosexuals came to our first services. They do today. At least twenty percent of our congregation is heterosexual. Their involvement is as great as anyone's.

When we had reached the three dozen mark, and we knew we were going to keep climbing and growing in membership, we knew we'd have to find a bigger place. People were sitting on the floor or standing around the walls. It often happens that way today.

Willie Smith and I went over to the Huntington Park

Women's Club to see if we couldn't rent space on Sundays for church services. They asked us what kind of people we were. We smiled, and said we were a church group. We wanted to rent their facilities. We were scared to death. Willie Smith was very charming to the ladies as we talked to them. He flattered one on the way her hair looked, and he talked about another's dress. When we got through, the women let us sign the lease for the building, and they said, "Okay! Great, you can use it." We started worshipping God there. We went from thirty-six to forty to forty-five, to right around fifty.

All at once an article appeared in *The Advocate*. When it did—and that was a move of God, too—attendance sky-rocketed. I want to tell you something, God works in strange, strange ways sometimes. We outgrew the lower floor of the Women's Club and had to move to their upstairs room. We finally started averaging around two hundred in that building.

We could rent the downstairs for social gatherings and for coffee house meetings after church. Our support from courageous people in the gay community kept up our zeal. We were really playing it all by ear. At one meeting shortly after we were in the Women's Club, a forceful articulate man spoke up after *The Advocate* editor had talked. This man said, "Tell us what *we* can do to help you." I told him that what I thought was needed most was some means of reaching out to everyone with our spiritual message couched in terms that would help change conventional attitudes about gay people. I insisted that gays had to change their attitudes about themselves, too. We had to walk proudly with God. Everyone had to respect that. I wanted to know more about the man I talked to. He seemed so confident and so eager to become involved. He introduced himself as John Hose, then he smiled and said, "The Reverend John Hose. My other half and I read about you in *The Advocate*. We had to come over today and see what you were up to. Curiosity brought us here. I think it will propel us forward into helping you in

some rather useful ways." That's how I met the man we call
Papa John. Was he useful and helpful to us! In less than two
weeks he was a member. A short time later he was on the
board of directors. In no time at all he was the assistant
pastor of the church. He brought a maturity and stability
that we sorely needed. He was not only an astute businessman, but one that young people could rely on for counseling. At that time he was one of the few people we had over
thirty. And that was a help. He had been a pastor back in
Ohio and Illinois somewhere. When he accepted his homosexuality, he gave up his ministry and became a very successful businessman. Now he's back pastoring where he
belongs.

Here's the typical story of one of the young people who
got involved in our church work at the same time that Papa
John did. He was a talented, black entertainer. He worked
with a large agency. He also read about us in that first big
feature story in *The Advocate.* Here is his story:

"I talked to two women I know, who are involved in the
same type of work. I showed them the newspaper. We were
intrigued by it. So we decided to band together, share our
bravery, and go. We did. At that time services were held in
the Huntington Park Women's Club, in the upstairs room.
There was no indication from the exterior that a church was
using the building. There were a lot of cars. There were
people milling about outside. We went in all of our bejew-
eled finery, of course. And we did feel slightly out of place,
but the greeters were so delighted to have us come. They
rushed up and said, 'Good morning, and welcome to Metropolitan Community Church.' That disarmed us, if that's
the word I'm looking for. We went in and were impressed
by the altar, the flowers; the whole scene was dignified. One
of the girls with me said that it looked formal to the point
of being Catholic. Then a slim, trim, short haired, Willie
Smith stepped up, and lead us in singing hymns. The hymns
were zestful, and really rocked the place. We anticipated the
processional. We had seen pictures of the Reverend Perry in

The Advocate. And when he walked down the aisle dressed in the black robe, and the white cassock, and sang the hymn at the top of his voice, it bowled us over. That shock of black hair, the piercing, smiling eyes and the puckish grin charmed us all.

"When the more solemn segments of the service, such as the pastoral and silent prayer, the gospel, and more hymns were behind us, the pastor came forth and said, 'If you love the Lord this morning, would you say, amen!' And a full-throated congregation, at full voice shouted back, 'Amen!' We could feel the thrill of being cast under this man's personal spell; his personal experience with God reached all of us. His sermon was a mixture. It was a kind of free-wheeling, hard-hitting, Southern Bible Belt, Pentecostal give 'em hell drive toward God. But it was also often quiet and tender and had an overall effect of being totally moving. He talked of love and dignity, and of our need to stand tall, and walk proud. He assured us that God walked with all of us. That's the way it must be for all of us. We must, therefore, walk with God. The girls with me were almost overcome. They were so touched that they have been unable to make an accommodation with their own former religions and guilt feelings. They have not returned. Nevertheless, I met Reverend Perry right after the service. He was sure he'd met me before. He'd seen me perform. I knew that I was back home with my religion. I've been back ever since. Mine was only a lapse of five years. I've seen others return after more than two decades, and piece out a new spiritual life for themselves."

In April of 1969 we were visited by some people who weren't really friendly to our community. I was told that they were plainclothes vice squad officers.

They had come by to look us over. A certain man was running for a certain public office in Los Angeles, and part of his campaign was to attack the gay community. The police had come at his behest. They tried to loiter in the rest rooms, if you can imagine that, in a church service. They must have thought that all homosexuals are just dying to make it in toilets. They waited, and did what vice squad officers do. They slouched around. They cruised. They grinned and winked at people. They rubbed their private parts, I presume they thought, invitingly. I sent our biggest, huskiest members of the congregation in to watch them. They were watched like they had never been before. We outnumbered them. So they got nowhere, and they finally left. It was just harassment, because we weren't in their jurisdiction. But, of course, they were police officers, so I suppose if it came down to it, they could have made a pinch. I explained to the congregation just what was going on, that we had visitors.

Now, I never tell anyone how to vote, but I did say that since that certain man was running, if anyone voted for him, they'd almost surely die and go to hell. We campaigned actively against him. And he lost. That was one of the first victories we had at the polls for our church and the rest of the gay community.

But the harassment was not over. It continued, and in a devious way that we were to become all too familiar with as time went on.

One day I went over to pick up my robes for a wedding. A member of the Women's Club met me, and she said, "I'd like to talk to you . . . . You people can't rent the building any more, after the next two weeks are up. You're paid up to then, and then that has to be it."

I said, "Why?"

She said, "Well, the janitor doesn't want to come in and work on Sundays." I went upstairs, and picked up my robes, and walked on out. I met her again, and I said, "Now, tell me something. What's the real reason?"

She just said, "Well, that's the reason we're giving."

And I said, "All right, God bless you. Thank you."

You know, it was really strange: the police chief there in Huntington Park was really very liberal. He was not at all concerned with the gay scene, unless it involved a juvenile, or unless force was involved. He didn't put his officers in public rest rooms waiting to arrest people. He was interested in keeping his police officers on the beat to patrol and keep down crimes of violence and burglaries. The police didn't go into any bars, either straight or gay, unless they were called. Then they usually went and waited outside, and the disturbers were brought out to them. So far as I know, that's still the policy there today. That gay bar is still going strong. It's a clean bar, no narcotics, just a friendly neighborhood watering place. That chief was aware of our church. Someone did ask him about Metropolitan Community Church. I'm told that he was asked what he thought of that bunch down there at the Women's Club. He is reported to have said, "To me it's just another denomination, as far as I'm concerned, and I just couldn't be bothered."

But here we were being ousted by a civic organization. We found later that someone from Los Angeles had told them that we were an undesirable homosexual organization, and that it was unwise to do business with that type of an outfit. They took the hint, and we were out. Once again, our congregation had to pack up robes, hymnals and all our property, and duck out like gypsies to look for a new place to hold church services. We had a lot of hymnals, because when Lou pointed out that we needed two hundred books, I appealed for a special collection. We got an enthusiastic response, too, there in Huntington Park. A lot of things happened there. We had a choir started. We had a sound system that began to grow and improve. We had moved up from a pump organ to an electric pipe organ. And that was only a few weeks away from absolutely nothing.

People who came were eager to pitch in. I think Willie Smith kind of personifies it. When we started he did suggest caution. He said, "Now, don't get too Catholic on me. I'm an old conservative and plain Seventh Day Adventist. But don't get too Pentecostal or I'll be unhappy in that direction. I just don't dig all that shouting and stamping and parading around. I just want to stay with two main rules: Love God, and help your fellow man. Keep the doctrine down to a mild roar, and avoid a lot of rules." He got a little free-wheeling, too, when he added his personal touch, The Singspiration. Before service, Willie spent half an hour or so leading the incoming congregation in hymns. It really warmed them all up. They loved it. They all just lit up and sang.

Even though we were being forced to pack up and move like political refugees one jump ahead of the Gestapo, I still had to find the time to do the really essential gut-work that I had to do to make the church live and grow. I'm talking about counseling, just being available for pastoral help whenever needed. Remember that we were new. The gay revolution was just getting under way. Most gay people were fighting it like it was a huge burdensome and shameful problem. I saw it as part of my job to reassure them that they were God's creatures, and human beings; gayness was just another factor in how they lived. The phone number for the church was the same as for my home. It was busy for counseling and appointments for advice and the resolution of pastoral matters. It rang as often as any emergency phone.

Many who called or came for counseling joined in our worship services—wherever held. I always tried to relieve the stress first and pray later. It's still that way in our church. If someone comes hungry to church, he is fed. Later we try to help him get his problems sorted out.

It was during June in 1969, when a personal incident brought about a change in my life. We had been filling up the Embassy Auditorium for about two weeks when a minister from another denomination wandered in to our meeting. He was looking for a different group. Someone was speaking at a coffee hour. I'll never forget the reaction that speech produced in this misdirected minister. He looked around to see if he could recognize a familiar face. Then he began to stare. The person speaking was a heterosexual transvestite who stopped to answer questions. There were a couple, and the questions and the answers hit this man so hard that he caved in. He just staggered out of that auditorium and went right upstairs. He made his way into the office and said, "Do you know what kind of group you've got worshipping down there?" And he managed to point a shaking finger toward the basement.

The manager said, "Why, it's a Christian group, I guess."

The minister recovered enough to say, "No, no, they can't be Christians! It's too terrible! They . . . they're perverts!" This minister didn't let matters rest. He rushed around the building, and on down to City Hall. He had a sympathetic audience.

We were told someone at City Hall phoned the Embassy management and asked if they were aware of what kind of group was meeting in the basement.

The lady said, "What kind of group?"

And the person calling said, "A homosexual group."

The manager said, "Yes, we're aware of that."

She was told by City Hall, "Well, we want them out of there. We're going to lease the building for an old folks home. It would be an advantageous time for you to get rid of them." We had one week to get out of the building.

We all began to scrounge around to find a new place to worship. I prayed hard. But just to help the good Lord to help us, I did a lot of scurrying to look for a more permanent place to hold services. This was on top of everything else. I still had counseling to do. And that phone kept going night and day. One thing that helped was subscribing to an answering service. This freed me of some of the work. Now I could control my time and energy.

One call on the service was from a Mr. Steve Jordan, who wanted information about the church. I finally got around to returning his call. As I recall the conversation ran something like this, "May I speak to Mr. Steve Jordan, please?

The voice said, "Hi, this is Steve."

I identified myself and said, "How may I help you?"

Mr. Jordan said, "Oh! Well . . . I've been reading this article in *The Advocate* see, and you say that you can be a

Christian and a homosexual, too. And I'd like to know how, according to the Bible, you can believe that?"

It was a fair question, one that I'm asked most often by most people, especially those I meet for the first time. I told Steve that it would really be impossible for me to answer his many questions on the phone, but if he was willing to meet me for pastoral counseling, I would do my best. He agreed. We made an appointment to meet in two days on June tenth in Sheri's, a Hollywood restaurant. At that time I was still paranoid about California's barbaric sex offense laws, so I had all my counseling appointments in public places.

On the evening of our date I sauntered into Sheri's. I ran into Willie Smith and a friend of his having dinner there. They insisted that I join them. I said I couldn't, I was going to meet a fellow that wanted to exchange views on the usual question. Willie said that they were going to leave in just a few minutes, and suggested I wait with them until my appointment arrived. He assured me that they'd leave right away, so I had nothing to worry about. In just a few minutes a young man walked up to the table, looked at my clerical garb, and asked, "Are you Reverend Perry? I'm Steve Jordan." I looked at him, and it made me nervous, upset, and uptight to do so. If ever there was a type that really turned me on here it was standing right in front of me. He was a young, wiry, small, American of Mexican descent. His hair was a luxurious shining coal black, almost blue, color. He had rather limpid dark brown eyes. His lips were full and sensuous. He had a rather impish grinning smile that won me completely. His skin was a flawless candy caramel color. I just went all watery inside. I think I managed to conceal my true state. I pulled myself together enough to introduce him to everyone else. He sat down. Willie and his friend finished their coffee, and left.

I urged Steve to tell me a little about himself. He was born here in Los Angeles in 1948. His parents had been married for two years when his mother discovered that she was pregnant. The pregnancy apparently prompted their separation. The split was bitter. Steve's mother wanted no part of anything that reminded her of the husband who had left her. When Steve was born she abandoned him. He was just five days old.

Steve was raised in a foster home in San Bernardino, California. His foster parents were former Mexican nationals who had emigrated in 1928. They still spoke only Spanish. It was the language of the Mexican barrio where they lived with other Latin American families.

There was one striking similarity Steve's background had with mine. He attended a Pentacostal church. The same rigid moral code obtained in Spanish just as it did in English.

Steve spoke only Spanish when he went to school. He just smiled whenever the teacher called upon him. She thought he was probably retarded, but it finally dawned on her that he didn't know any English. Steve had a rough time in school getting the languages sorted out.

When he was fifteen Steve's foster parents told him that he wasn't their real son. That shattered him emotionally, so he rebelled. He had no answers as to the whys of his life, and he started to withdraw into himself. He dropped out of church, and turned his back on most of the barrio (ghetto) culture in which he had grown up.

During his last year of high school he discovered that he was gay. He had no real overt experiences; he just knew he was different.

After high school he left San Bernardino to come to Los Angeles and go to college. He read about Metropolitan Community Church while he was a student. Lots of people do.

We talked about what the Bible does and does not say about homosexuality. I explained how it has been used to prove and disprove practically everything. I gave him my own personal views and said I'd see him in church the following Sunday at the Embassy Auditorium, but he should be sure and make it because we didn't know where we'd be after Sunday. He said that he'd see me.

He did. I saw him in the hall before the start of service. He'd been constantly on my mind since I'd met him. I wanted to date him—for real—so I went up to him, and asked, "What are you going to be doing today after church?"

He just smiled that impish, boyish grin of his and said, "Well, I didn't have anything planned, but Willie asked me to go out with him for coffee right after service."

I said, "You tell Willie *you* are going out with *me!*"

I hadn't even had a date with Steve, and I was already jealous. My tone showed it, because he looked up at me and grinned again, and said, "Okay." He moved in with me the next week and it's been okay ever since.

At services the next Sunday I said, "You know we move around so much that if you don't come every time you might just lose us for awhile. You'll hear from us, but we don't want you to miss out on anything.

One of our friends came forward. This friend was a member of the First Methodist Church. He went to that organization and asked if we could meet there. He said, "Look here's a group of Christians that need a place to meet. Can they possibly meet here?"

They said, "Sure, for one week." We did, but they extended our run for another week while we were desperately looking for a place.

Even in Huntington Park, some of us had thought about either buying a church or buying a piece of land and trying to build. We felt that permanent even then. We kept pressing for that. One time we had gone out to look at a small church over near a junkyard. It was a pretty little church, and the price was right, but it only seated seventy-five. We talked that over, and we went back, and looked. I said, "Well, we'll pray about it on Sunday, and God will give us the answer." That next Sunday we had over ninety in attendance. That was our answer.

Everything seemed to be closed to us. We were growing, but we were still total outcasts. No church would let us use their facilities, neither would the civic groups, nor the places with auditoriums that fit our needs.

Finally, Willie Smith said, "Well, why don't we try going into the Encore Theater, the movie house where I work?" So, once again, we got all done up in our Sunday best. We called upon the owner-manager, Mr. Louis Federici. Willie said, "Look, we're a church group, and we need a place to meet for about four or five weeks until we find a permanent home. Would you permit us to rent the theater?" Mr. Federici is a Catholic, and he certainly is a generous Christian. He let us have his theater, rent free. For the time we were there, we added over six thousand dollars to our building fund. We were there for over a year and a half. Other theater owners told Mr. Federici that they were going to take up a collection so he could put stained glass windows in his theater auditorium.

He was a lot more full of the spirit of Christianity than most other churchgoers or Christian groups we had encountered. He told us that day, when Willie and I went to find out about the use of his theater, that he knew he would give it to us for nothing. He laughed, as we did, when we said, "Well, that's a really good price for it."

Our growth rate was astronomical enough to be a phenomenon. But it wasn't the novelty of the church, nor people coming to get religion that accounted for all of it. We had a clear vision of our mission to start with, and we had a social action program from the start. Part of the social action was party time. But the most important part was really helping homosexuals with jobs, housing, problems about being homosexuals, acceptance problems and clubs in which they could find a place. We wanted to give them places to meet and activities that they could work out together, and we did.

I remember our first real social over in the Huntington Park Women's Club. We didn't really know how it would work out. Should we have dancing, which is illegal between people of the same sex in Los Angeles? Should we serve beer? What kind of food should we serve? These seem like simple enough problems, but then it was like opening a can of worms. We decided that we would dance. Period.

Our first May festival was a complete sell-out. It was sensational. We had a floor show with musicians, singers, impersonators, and a wild sing-in by everybody. We raised over a thousand dollars which we needed for rent and to get our social action program going. We had to give people food, clothing, and find housing for them. The May Festival may have raised some eyebrows around the Women's Club. And I think it also helped us need to find new quarters faster.

The church business and social action were conducted from my home in Huntington Park. That phone number must have been the hottest in town. Everyone was calling. They wanted information; they wanted counseling. Some thought we were a call-boy service. Some really desperately needed help. We never hung up. We played it by ear, and we talked to people. One young man called one time and was so depressed he was planning to commit suicide. Well, there it was in the middle of the night. I got Willie Smith up, and we drove over and talked to him. He found that someone cared. We helped him. And he's been an active member ever since.

That started our Crisis Intervention Committee. Volunteers came forward to man the phone around the clock. Others stood by to go out and see what they could do to help. We began to get training from professionals who could help us in suicide prevention, and in counseling for acceptance. This can all be related to that first sermon, "Be True To You."

That brought in people like Professor Dank, who helped us lay out a social program. We had excellent contacts with local agencies. Civil servants came forward to help us. They remained anonymous, for the most part. Lawyers became available for consultation, and for the minimum of legal fees. We worked very closely with the Probation Department, with Human Resources, with all areas of the United

States Health, Education and Welfare Department, and on all local and state arms of that area of work.

I appointed the first board of directors, and I also appointed the first deacons. They were just there, and they were willing workers. They helped become the arms and legs of the church to go and help people, and bring them for pastoral and professional counseling. They took food and clothing to people.

Our deacons started school. Reverend Richard Ploen and I held classes. These became the seminary classes where we trained deacons, exhorters, licensed ministers. And we had been able, then, to ordain some who had finished the entire course of study. We drew ministers and deacons from other churches. They transferred their license or degrees and credits, and their ordination certificates to our church.

Many who came felt that we were holding together a really diverse organization. People came from all over, from every race, creed, color, national origin. One day, at the Encore, a rather large gentleman came forward and said, "I am a lapsed High Church Episcopalian, whatever that means. And I came here to see what kind of fraud was being perpetrated. I had read about you and the church in *The Advocate*. I really came to sneer. But I am stunned to see your congregation made up of Catholics, all Protestant sects, and Jews. Truly, MCC means Catholic and even more than that." That man was Bill Thorne, who hasn't missed a Sunday since then. He joined the choir, became a deacon, and is now chairman of the board of deacons. I've never seen anyone give of himself so generously to helping the oppressed who have come to us. But he's only one of many.

Reverend Richard Ploen began classes for the deaf, and classes for others who wanted to learn the sign language of the deaf and mute. We had a section where that group sat and followed a leader, not only in the service and prayer, but in singing hymns. We even formed a silent choir; not all the members were deaf or mute, and they just stayed with that interesting and enlightening program.

We were gathering strength even from the people who ignored us or tossed us out of our church homes. Every time someone asked us to move, it only brought us new people. One such young man came because he heard of the church in a gay bar. He was an agnostic, but he came, and heard the voice of the Lord. He studied, and became a licensed minister. He went to San Francisco and started a mission there. It's become the second largest congregation in the Fellowship of Metropolitan Community Churches. The young man, Howard Wells, went recently to New York to open our mission there. He's a bright and eager young man, and his drive will just not be stopped.

Our first great test of courage came, I think, when we were nine months old. We were asked to stand up and be counted, to stand for homosexual civil rights. We hadn't thought seriously about a group effort until then. We'd talked to a lot of people, we'd bailed them out, and we'd fought job discrimination, and so on. But we got a call from the San Francisco Committee for Homosexual Freedom. It was in April 1969. The committee wanted us to demonstrate in front of the Los Angeles offices of States Steamship Lines. In San Francisco they had fired a young man because he was a homosexual, and he admitted it. They found out by reading the *Berkeley Barb.* One young man was shown with his arm around another. It was just an informal pose of camaraderie. They both publicly stated that they were homosexuals. One was a very active militant for gay rights up there, and he had a picket line going up there at States Steamship. Would we join in? Would we put our people on the streets here and start fighting for fair employment for gay people?

I knew that we would. But I had never asked anyone to really go out and hit the streets and really fight back. It was going to be hard. There weren't a lot of us, and most were working at that hour. But we were to demonstrate during the noon hour in front of the Mobil Building in downtown Los Angeles. We numbered only eight, and we didn't know what would happen. We were afraid of the unknown, but we knew that for us it was a crucial test.

Wednesday, at 11:30 in the morning, we gathered with placards that we had made. The placards denounced States Steamship Lines for its employment policies. We also had some that stated a person's efficiency had nothing to do with his sexual orientation, as had been demonstrated in all professions, business, the arts, and the military services.

So we marched. I was dressed in my most conservative dark suit, with a clerical collar. It sure didn't take us long to find out how "they" were going to react to us. During that first lunch break, when people came out of the building by the hundreds, we got some really cold stares. One person near me said, "Oh, my God, the fairies have flown down from Hollywood." They jeered at us. We heard words like queers, faggots, fairies, sissies—words I'd forgotten—and some words that I'm not even going to use in print. We didn't reply. We just marched on determinedly. We smiled back. Once in awhile, I would say, "God bless you, sir, or God bless you, madam." But we kept marching in a very orderly file up and down.

Upstairs in that building someone took offense, and bags of water started dropping down from the roof of the building. Have you ever been hit with a bag of water? It can knock you out. But either their aim was bad or God kept us out of the way. The water bombs only hit the businessmen and women walking in and out of the building. The water bombs raised hell with all of the spectators. We just marched on and never looked up, and we passed out our leaflets.

The second day was just like the first one. We were threatened. We were vilified. We were bombed, but not so much. I think the gentlemen whose suits were all messed up with the water aided us materially by putting a stop to that.

Day number three was something else. By this time, some of the people were making friends with us. They stopped and talked, and we had a lot more backbone, too. We weren't afraid of anything or anybody. We explained a lot to everyone who stopped and talked. A lot of people did. Well, you know that thing about pride going before a fall. I looked up as proud as all get out, and I saw this lady coming determinedly up the street. I held out a leaflet and said, "Here, madam, would you take one of our leaflets?" She didn't say a word. She just hauled off and hit me as hard as she could with her purse. I didn't believe it. So, like a fool, I repeated myself. I said, "Madam, are you *sure* you don't want one of our leaflets?" So, she hit me again.

She said, "If I had my way all of you perverted individuals would be locked up, in jail, and the key thrown away!"

I said, "Madam, that's a wonderful Christian attitude you have."

She looked me over, backed off a step, and I thought she was going to hit me again. She said, "Young man, do you know what the Book of Leviticus says?"

I told her, "I sure do! It says that it's a sin for a woman to wear a red dress, for a man to wear a cotton shirt and woolen pants at the same time, for anyone to eat shrimp, oysters, or lobster—or your steak too rare."

She said, "That's not what I mean!"

I said, "I know that's not what you mean, Honey, but you forgot all of these other dreadful sins, too, that are in the same book of the Bible."

She said, "Do you know what Saint Paul said?"

Again, I said, "I sure do. He said for women to be silent, not to speak."

She said, "That's not what I mean either."

I said, "I know it's not, Honey, but Paul disliked women: he said that women were not to teach, preach, and that they were not to have *any* sort of authority over a man. Where would our women's liberation groups be, if they had listened to the Apostle Paul? He didn't like women with short hair, nor men with long hair. He said, 'If a man have long hair, it is a shame unto him, but if a woman have long hair, it is her glory.' Are we going to close the doors of the church just because the Apostle Paul didn't like women with short hair, nor men with long hair?"

She said, "That's still not what I meant." I pressed on; I said, "I know it's not, Honey, but you know Paul was a very generous fellow. He met a slave one time, and the word of God says that he converted this slave, made him a happy *Christian* slave, whatever *that* is. Well, he didn't try to get him to Canada via the Underground Railroad. He sent him back to his master *still a slave!* Paul wasn't against slavery. You know he was cited as the principal reason for the Southern Baptists to split away from their church in 1845, and found their organization, just so they could keep their slaves. Yet, today, no one in his right mind would quote the Apostle Paul to justify his right to maintain slaves or slavery."

Then she took out of that heavy purse a small, but hefty, Bible. She said, "Read this, and see what Paul said to the Romans."

Well, some think I never passed my examinations at that Bible college I went to, but I did. I shut her Bible and handed it back to her and I recited from memory exactly what he said in chapter 1, verses 26-28. I said, "Here they are, madam: Paul's Epistle To The Romans, chapter 1, verses 26-28:

For this cause God gave them up unto vile affections. For even their women did change the natural use into that which is against nature: And likewise also the men, leaving the natural use of the woman, burned in their lust one toward another; men with men working that which is unseemly, and receiving in themselves that recompense of their error which was meet. And even as they did not like to retain God in *their* knowledge, God gave them over to a reprobate mind, to do those things which are not convenient. . . .

"And in First Corinthians, chapter 6, verse 9.

> Know ye not that the unrighteous shall not inherit the
> kingdom of God? Be not deceived; neither fornicators,
> nor idolators, nor adulterers, nor effeminate, nor abus-
> ers of themselves with mankind. . . .

"And further, in First Timothy, chapter 1, verses 9 and 10:

> Knowing this, that the law is not made for a righteous
> man, but for the lawless and disobedient, for the un-
> godly and for sinners, for unholy and profane, for mur-
> derers of fathers, and murderers of mothers, for
> manslayers, for whoremongers, for them that defile
> themselves with mankind, for men-stealers, for liars,
> for perjured persons, and if there be any other thing
> that is contrary to sound doctrine. . . .

"And I'll agree, madam, Paul did not like homosexuals,
but Paul did not take to women's rights, and he would be
appalled at short hair on a woman, or excessively long hair
on a man. Now, if we're going to close the doors of the
churches to the hippies just because they have long hair, and
to women who have short hair, or wear a red dress, or eat
those forbidden foods, or who teach, or preach, or who
exercise *any* sort of authority over a man, where would we
be?"

She said, "All right, smarty, what did Jesus say?"

I said, "Now, according to the way you think and act He
would have been a real weirdy—for you. If He lived in this
day and age, the way you people label individuals, you
would have labeled *Him* a homosexual right off the bat! I
don't believe that Jesus was a homosexual. But I know you
people. Here was a guy that was raised by a mother with no
father—typical of the homosexual syndrome, according to
so many psychiatrists (for what's that's worth)—He never
married, and ran around with twelve guys all the time. Not

only that, He wasn't above having bodily contact with another man: John the Beloved lay on the breast of Jesus at the Last Supper. Not only that, but a *guy* betrayed Him with a kiss! Doesn't that make you want to throw up? Not once did Jesus say, 'Come unto me, all ye heterosexuals—who have sex in the missionary position with a member of the *opposite* sex—and you can become true followers.' No! Jesus said, 'Come unto me, all ye that labour, and are heavy laden, and I will give you rest.' And that includes homosexuals, too. God does not condemn me for a sex drive that He has created in me. He doesn't condemn me unless I leave the areas of love and go into the areas of destructive, excessive lust."

Well, she was as white as a sheet. She just stood there staring at me. I went right on, "When Jesus was asked what is the great commandment, Jesus didn't talk about homosexuality or heterosexuality. He said this, 'And thou shalt love the Lord thy God with all thy heart, and with all thy soul, and with all thy mind, and with all thy strength: And the Second is like unto the First, 'Thou shalt love thy neighbor as thyself.' And I think that's the gospel according to Jesus Christ. If I follow the Word, and those gospels, and I am brought to God and saved from my sins, not saved from my natural sexuality, then I believe I am a Christian and I am saved.

"While we're at it, in Romans, chapter 14, verse 14, it says, 'I know, and am persuaded by the Lord Jesus, that *there is* nothing unclean of itself: but to him that esteemeth any thing to be unclean, to him it is *unclean.*' And in Titus, chapter 1, verse 15, it says, 'Unto the pure all things *are* pure: but unto them that are defiled and unbelieving *is* nothing pure!' "

She turned and left without another word, still as white as a sheet, and rather shaken and trembling.

After that first demonstration, we picked up a lot of support. People read about us in *The Advocate* again. They picked up our pamphlets, they came in, and they called in.

Actually, our demonstration then and the one in San Francisco were the real beginnings of Gay Liberation as it is today. They were nonviolent. They were the kind of passive resistance and civil disobedience that both Mahatma Gandhi and Dr. Martin Luther King had advocated and used so effectively. In our case, the man did not get his job back; he had no hearing; the company just refused to talk to him, or to any of us. He remained unemployed for some time and then did part-time work. It took a great effort to get him a job that came anywhere near his former job and salary. We had lost a battle, but our line was drawn. We had also recruited a number of people to our cause. That was most important.

We discovered, however, the large number of similar cases of people who were fired because they were found to be gay. We turned up a file of cases of needless police harassment and police brutality.

Not all members of my church felt as I did, that we had to take a militant, nonviolent stand against the kind of dehumanizing brutality and harassment we were up against. But those of us who had been through it knew that we would never be pushed again without standing up for our rights. We would never stand in the shadows. We would never hide our faces again. We would stand in the sunshine. We would stand with our heads held high, never again bowed low. We would know that God was with us, and that we were His children. We were on His side. We would never again be afraid of what society could do to us.

People sometimes ask me, "Aren't you a little worried? Aren't you just a little scared? There are a lot of people in this world, and in this state, and hereabouts who don't like homosexuals. Aren't you afraid that someone will some day physically attack you or some of your followers?" Well, of course, that's on my mind. And the fact that something could actually happen to someone else does bother me. But I think that, like me, they have learned that that's a chance we must take. It's a chance worth taking. You know we have had to take that same stride down that lonely trail that our black brothers and sisters have been taking these past years. We have to go on even if they turn the vicious dogs loose upon us as they did on the blacks in Alabama, and in other places in the deep South. We have to go on and survive that and push forward. You know that, once you wake up and know that you are an oppressed person. You must know first that you are a human being, and you must learn that you have your rights, too, and they don't mean anything unless you're willing to fight for them.

Meanwhile, my mother had come back from Florida. Steve and I insisted that she do so. I wanted her to come and live with me because I was afraid that once the church got really started, she would be put down by members of her family, or by her friends back in Florida. Most important though was the debt I owed her. She had sacrificed everything for her sons, and especially for me. I realized that I had pushed her into making such hard sacrifices for us when I had run away from home at the age of thirteen. She had done anything, taken any job, just to hold her family together and to educate her sons. She did it. Three of us went to college. The fourth dropped out, but he picked up extension courses along the way to fill out his education. I felt that it was my turn to take care of my mother. While she lives with me, she goes and spends a month or so with the others when it is mutually convenient. But she works beside me. She, Steve, and I shared our home, and with a minimum of mother-in-law problems, too.

All this time we had been looking for a building which would serve as a church office and parsonage. We finally found an old house at 1149-1/2 North Virgil Avenue in Los Angeles. It was just north of Santa Monica Boulevard, near the junction that street makes with Sunset Boulevard. It was a really beat up ramshackle structure, barely habitable, but we got it for a good price. I took Steve over to see it, and he almost had a heart attack. "You want us to live in that?" was all he could bring himself to say. It was all we could afford. That was the reality of the situation.

Over forty eager members and friends of our church turned out, determined to make our new quarters livable. The disheartening old firetrap had seventeen rooms, but we got out paint, hammers and all the tools it took, and we did get it going. We finally moved in on a hot August 29, 1969. We had a base to operate from. It was quite a home. Reverend Ploen wanted it as a halfway house so that we could provide emergency housing for periods of up to three days, a place where we could have meetings, classes, choir practice, publications, and church administration. It was far too small from the day we moved in. It went day and night. We had a counseling office, and our crisis Hot Line manned twenty-four hours per day. Then we had emergency drop-ins, and those we went out and scooped up. Church business, classes, students, people waiting, and the crisis line personnel, plus our emergency cases were all under foot. It got to be just too much for the family life we were trying to hold together. Steve, Mom, and I needed a private life. We lived in that house for over nine months, a lot longer than we had ever thought we would. I blessed the day when I could move us all to an apartment and turn that ramshackle, tumble-down house over to the church.

Certainly, in the back of my mind, was the sure knowledge that we would have our own church home. It was essential. And, whenever I could, I searched for one. All of us began to do just that. But it was nowhere in sight. It would take a good deal more action on our part, more work and more growth.

Sometimes I am moved to action on the spur of the moment. I take my inspiration from whatever impulse comes over me on any given occasion. On Flag Day, June 14, 1970, I stunned my congregation, irritated some of my board of directors, and set off on a crusade that is still going on. I was determined, as a loyal American, to embark upon a fast until we had a really meaningful dialogue about changing the unjust laws that are used to harass and discriminate against homosexuals. These laws are in effect in most states. They are usually vague, sweeping, holdovers from the Middle Ages, reenforced by the Victorian period. In California, almost anything between two men can be described as lewd and lascivious conduct, and all forms of sexual activity, even between consenting adults, is restricted to copulation in the face to face missionary position. Oral copulation is a felony. So is anal copulation. Any embrace, kissing or suggestive gesture, touch or unseemly remark is a misdemeanor. Jails in the metropolitan areas have scores of people in them who have been imprisoned for periods up to six months for each offense. In addition, they are required to pay fines of up to five hundred dollars. For repeated offenders, or for felonies, the threat of the sex offender's prison at Atascadero looms. There, one can be sent for an indeterminate sentence, and when and if one is released, one can then be sent back to a state facility to serve another sentence. At Atascadero, shock treatment, chemical therapy, aversion therapy and the like are practiced against unwilling prisoners. It is a living hell equal to bedlam, or worse.

Anyone convicted of any of these sex offenses must register as a sex offender. The conviction and registration carry a lifetime stigma that changes the person's entire life. He is automatically ineligible for most civil service jobs. If he has a license to work in many businesses or professions, he loses that license. These fields of work range from a hairdresser, through barber, bartender, manicurist, masseur, teacher, professor, nurse, therapist, lawyer and almost anything calculated to bring the victim of this registration or conviction into contact with the general public. The punishment is a lifetime of disaster for those who have been caught in these victimless crimes, who have desired to love people of their own sex. A key point in our mission is to abolish these laws, either through court proceedings or by legislative action. Meanwhile, we want to have the enforcement cease being so discriminatory against the gay community, especially against homosexual males. We think that it is a terrible waste of the taxpayers money. A former mayor of a large California city said recently that he found it a great waste, and he advocated that other succeeding mayors do what he did: put the cops back on the beat preventing crimes of violence.

It was essential that we start a dialogue with those in government on all levels, on whatever level, as soon as possible. Recently, Hugh Heffner, the editor of *Playboy* has established a foundation to fight for changes in legislation. He is a welcome ally, for our goals are the same in this matter.

When I had decided to fast and to force the issue of a dialogue, I did it in a spirit of patriotism. It was inspired by Flag Day. I didn't advise nor ask the board of directors. I should have, but I felt the urgency so keenly that I didn't take the time. Some knew before I went before the congregation. Some said, "Wait!" Others said, "We're with you all the way!" So I found myself in the Encore Theater, where we had had standing room only for over a year. It was Sunday, June 14th, Flag Day. After my announcements, the choir sang as it usually did. As I started into my sermon, I asked everyone to follow along in their Bibles with me as I read the Beatitudes, "Please turn to Matthew, chapter 5, and start to read with me, commencing at the first verse:

> And seeing the multitudes, he went up into a mountain: and when he was set, his disciples came unto him. And he opened his mouth, and taught them, saying, Blessed *are* the poor in spirit: for *theirs* is the kingdom of heaven. Blessed *are* they that mourn: for they *shall* be comforted. Blessed *are* the meek: for they *shall* inherit the earth. Blessed *are* they which do hunger and thirst after rightousness; for they *shall* be filled. Blessed *are* the merciful: for they *shall* obtain mercy. Blessed *are* the pure in heart: for *they shall* see God. Blessed *are* the peacemakers: for *they shall* be called the children of

God. Blessed *are* they which are persecuted for righteousness' sake: for theirs *is* the kingdom of heaven. Blessed *are* ye when *men* shall revile you, and persecute *you,* and shall say all manner of evil against you falsely, for my sake. Rejoice and be exceeding glad: for great *is* your reward in heaven: for so persecuted they the prophets which were before you."

I prayed and asked the congregation to be seated as I preached.

"In the book, Matthew, that I read from, 'Blessed are ye ...' Jesus said, when He was teaching the disciples, or, in most new translations, 'Happy are the pure in heart,' or 'Happy are the meek.' You know, God's children should be the happiest on earth. I've said this before many, many times. When you've got that old time religion way down deep in your heart, as we Pentecostals say, you should be happy. My religion makes me happy. It doesn't make me sad. As I've said, you don't want to look like the Missouri mule eating briars, you want to look like the sons of a king or the daughters of a king, because you have something to be happy about.

"Many, many times I remember the story about the woman at a Pentecostal camp meeting. And I think maybe I've shared this with you before. You know at camp meetings, the people get happy, and they praise the Lord, and they glorify the Lord. It's a time of rejoicing. I remember a camp meeting in the Church of God. Every year we would gather in Birmingham, Alabama. There'd be about five thousand of us. And every year we'd have speakers, speakers going all day long. Different preachers. One would finish, we'd break for lunch, and another one would start. And then we'd break for supper, and somebody else would start that night. Services would go on until after midnight. People gathered around the altars, praised the Lord, and just had a good time. And you know, I can remember when people were very emotional. I know we used to have people

in the Pentecostal church sitting on those old benches that
were so sliverish that you'd expect them to fall apart. And,
yet, some lady would get happy and jump up and start to
walk the backs of those benches. Now why they wouldn't
fall apart or fall over with her would always be beyond me.

"I remember one time, a sister got real happy, got to
shouting, shouted up to a great big fan, backed up into it,
and you recall that our women didn't cut their hair. I remember this fan just grabbed her right by the hair. And she
shouted right back into that thing. And her hair was so long
and so thick that it bogged the works, jammed up that fan
—just before it scalped her. But she was happy!

"Well, the sister was in something of a state. But one of
the camp meeting speakers heard her say, 'Woo, Praise the
Lord. Woo, thank You Lord for the devil. Woo, thank You
Lord for the devil.' Finally, his curiosity got the better of
him. He kept hearing her say, 'Thank You Lord for the
devil.' He moved in close; he thought he was misunder
standing her, what the woman was saying. Finally, he got in
close enough, and sure enough that's what she was saying
all right, 'Woo, thank You Lord for the devil.'

"So he poked her in the side, and said, 'Sister, we're here
to save you from sin, and to cast the devil out. And you're
thanking God for the devil. Why in the world are you doing
that?'

"And she said, 'Well, if he keeps on chasin' me like he's
chasin' me now, he's going to run me right into heaven.'

"So, I guess sometimes that's the way it is. We should be
happy. I'm real happy. This last week, my lover and I cele-
brated our first anniversary. And I said, 'Well, we'll do it
joyously. We're going to reenact the scene. I'm going to take
you out to supper. We're going to have a good time.' So I
told him I'd decided to take him back to Sheri's where I met
him. He didn't go for the idea, especially when I told him
that I was going to have Willie Smith and Wayne, who were
with me that night. So we went out alone, and we were
happy. We had a good time that evening, came back home

and went to sleep! I'm thankful that God makes us this happy.

"Well, that's the God I serve—He makes me happy. I look today at the flag. I think you know that today is Flag Day. And I'm happy that I'm an American. I am. There's a lot of bad things in this country. But the good still outweighs the bad as far as I'm concerned. And I look at the flag and it means something to me. Now, maybe it doesn't to other people. I've been accused sometimes of being really a member of the establishment. And in some ways I guess I am, and I don't apologize for that. But I happen to love this old country of ours, and I'm thankful I am an American. I have the freedom of speech, and I'm thankful because God makes me happy.

"This last week I had the most interesting experience, I think that I've had in my life up to this point. We've made application for a parade permit—as most of you know. We're going to have a joyous celebration, not a demonstration. A celebration. We wanted to just march as homosexuals who are citizens—full citizens—of this country. We want to reaffirm that.

"Well, we went to the police commission. When we got there, we met a policeman. He informed us that our hearing wouldn't come up 'til about three o'clock. So, if we wanted to leave, we could. He informed us that the police commission was having lunch with the parks commission, and they were going to be late in getting started. Well, we went and had a cup of coffee. We came back about 2:15, and they'd already passed everything on the agenda. Except us. And when we got there, they asked me to act as spokesman for our group before the commission. I was shocked. I didn't know the chief of police of the city of Los Angeles was going to be there. He was sitting on one side. They asked me to stand up, and the president of the commission asked me my name and what church I pastored. The commissioners knew exactly what church I pastored. They started questioning me.

"Now, I know what Daniel felt like when he walked into the den of lions. It seems like an eternity. I was actually standing in front of them less than an hour. But I have never in all my life felt anything quite like it. I know now what a minority individual feels like. We kept talking. And, finally, Chief Davis spoke up. He said, "Did you know that homosexuality is illegal in the state of California?'

"I looked at him, and I said, 'No sir, it's not.' We then debated the issue.

"And he said, 'Well, I want to tell you something. As far as I'm concerned, granting a parade permit to a group of homosexuals to parade down Hollywood Boulevard would be the same as giving a permit to a group of thieves and robbers.'

"I thanked him for being so honest. Finally, the motion was made. And one commissioner said, 'There'll be violence in the streets.'

"Well, I remember that Captain Wesley of the Hollywood Division said the same thing about the first Gay-In that the Gay Liberation Front sponsored. And he said, 'Around five o'clock violence will start in that park.' And around five o'clock the law moved in and started making arrests. That was the violence.

"They debated among themselves. The commission was against it, but they said, 'We're going to give the permit, if you can post two bonds. One in the amount of one million dollars. One in the amount of five hundred thousand dollars. And if you will post in cash the amount of fifteen hundred dollars, in cash—that amount—to pay the policemen that it will take to protect you. And, you must have at *least* three thousand people marching. If not you go to the sidewalks.' I thanked them.

"As I said, I had never felt so funny in all my life. And when I left that place I had to cry. I felt, oh Lord, You know it's pretty bad. I'm just a human being. But what I do in bed colors everything these people think about me. But you know something, we didn't give up. When it starts getting rough, that's when I work the best. And I tell you that my God is bigger than the Los Angeles Police Department. He's bigger than the state of California. He's bigger than the United States Government.

"We called the American Civil Liberties Union, and they have entered the case. We're going to hold that parade! June the 28th!

"You know, many times when we have our beach parties everybody cuts up with me. I put on my bathing suit, I go running out to get into the surf. And they say, 'Ah, the pastor is fixing to practice walking on water.' Well, I want to tell you something. The Lord literally helped me walk on water this last week. And that was the water of prejudice and the water of hate. He didn't let me sink down. I didn't have to get down there with them! I held my head high, and I know everything is going to work out.

"I'm not afraid, because I'm happy! I know that God's right there, and He's making me the happy person that I am! He's making you happy. You've all got something to smile about this morning.

"After this happened, I prayed. I said to the Lord, I want to do something. I'm tired! It's been almost two years. And we've worked so hard. Nothing's been changed so far. Nothing! People are hearing about us, but nothing's been changed. Lord, You help me. I want to do something. I want to let people know we're here. Not for Troy Perry's self-glory, but for Yours, oh Lord.

"June the 28th, after the parade, I'm starting a *fast*. And I'm sitting down on a corner on Hollywood Boulevard. And I'm going to stay there and fast as long as it takes. If it's ten days, twenty days, thirty days. 'Til somebody comes and talks, and lets us know that at least there're some state or federal officials that are interested in seeing something happen. And I need your prayers. I can't do it alone. I know my God is able. He'll see me through this thing somehow. And I want you to know this—this morning I'm happy. These are tears of joy that I shed. 'Cause I *know my God is able!*''

We knew that a turning point had been reached. Their prayers and hearts were with me. All knew that I would not turn back. From the outset, I had explained that our way would not be easy. It would be hard. The Lord would try us many times and in many ways. This was one of these trials. We would again be weighed in the balance, and we would again come up winners. We would not be found wanting.

As we left the services that day, many shook my hands and warmly touched me, embraced me, and wished me well. Some insisted upon joining me. I asked them to wait until our action could be well planned. But they should keep in touch.

The next day, I went down to the American Civil Liberties Union for some advice. They supplied us with an attorney, Mr. Herbert Selwynn. He studied the case, and said he would be honored to appear at the police commission with me a week later. The police commission dropped all of its specifications except the requirement that we pay one thousand five hundred dollars for police protection. That was to protect us from the hard hats that might attack us. Well, I said, I didn't know any hard hats in Hollywood. So we left. That was on Friday.

On Monday we went to the California Superior Court and asked for, and were granted, a court order that not only granted us the parade permit, but required the police to provide us with whatever protection would be required to maintain an orderly parade. In making his ruling, the judge said that we were all citizens of the state of California and entitled to equal protection under its laws. We would not pay any extra taxes or fees to the Los Angeles Police Department, and they were ordered to protect us as they would any other group.

We had exactly two days to throw a parade together. Every gay organization in town wanted to participate, but no one was really prepared. None thought we'd ever get the permit. Once we had it, we went into action. I don't know where all the paraphernalia of the floats and parade exhibits came from, but a lot of runners must have run through garages, attics, display houses, costume houses and who knows what all. It was decided to hold the parade with the various groups marching down Hollywood Boulevard from the assembly area near Hollywood and Highland Avenue. We would march east to Vine Street and then return to our starting point. No gay group or conglomeration of gay groups, had ever gotten this far before.

As we were forming for the parade, we learned that our gay brothers and sisters in New York had failed to get their permit, and had to march on the sidewalks without any formation. We were exultant to learn that they had gone on and marched anyway to their Gay-In up in Central Park.

We couldn't get the bands we wanted to have, nor the horsemen, nor a lot of the floats, but we did exceptionally well anyway. The parade started with Willie Smith driving his VW Microbus, and playing some recordings of World War II German marches over an amplification system he had hooked up. Right behind him was the Society of Anubis, a social group of the hinterlands. They owned a retreat house out in the San Bernardino Mountains. And here they were, militant conservatives, going down Hollywood Boulevard with a float and the goddess of Anubis on a white stallion.

The alphabetical order was a little haphazard. Behind the Anubis section was *The Advocate* float bedecked with a carload of groovy guys in bikini swim suits. This was a mass of muscle calculated to turn everyone on. It did. After the male beauties, all fresh from their triumph at their annual contest, the parade ran the gamut of just about anything you could name. I think Focus was next. This is a pretty conservative gay group from extremely conservative Orange County. The Focus group carried a large sign reading "Homosexuals for Ronald Reagan." I heard one woman spectator on the sidewalk say, "I can forgive them for being homosexuals, but not for being for Ronald Reagan."

Gay Liberation came marching down the street carrying banners and shouting, "Two, four, six, eight—gay is just as good as straight." That drew two kinds of comments from the sidewalk crowd. One was an enthusiastic echo, the other derision. But the marchers were followed by the chilling spectacle of a Gay Lib float with a young beautiful man fastened on a cross. Above him a large black and white banner was emblazoned with the words, "In Memory of Those Killed by the Pigs." Reaction to that was a silent shock wave that stunned and chilled all the spectators. To turn the mood back to the festive occasion there was also a Gay Lib Guerrilla Theatre. This was a flock of shrieking drag queens all wearing gauzy pastel dresses, and running every which way to escape club wielding guys dressed as cops and sporting large badges with the word "Vice" splashed across them.

Another organization marching with us was a group of friends carrying a large sign reading, "Heterosexuals for Homosexual Freedom." It was a direct, welcome, and reassuring gesture. This is happening oftener, but we need a lot more of it.

A fife and drum accompanied the flag. There were drag queens. One section that particularly amused me was the pet section. Pets were carried, led, and pushed; some were in cages, some in highly decorated cases. Topping that off, one fellow had a big white husky dog on a leash. He had a sign on his dog reading, "All of us don't walk poodles." There was a motorcycle group in black leather led by a butch young man resplendent in black leather jacket, pants, gloves, and dripping with chains that seemed to encrust his heavy costume. To set this off in a frolicsome mood he wore pink high-heeled shoes.

Pat Rocco's group, SPREE (Society of Pat Rocco Enlightened Enthusiasts), had a large number of colorfully costumed people, many carrying SPREE signs and slogans about gay films. Several wildly decorated cars also carried SPREE girls and many handsome young men who had appeared in Pat's films. The whole SPREE group was preceded by an enormous lavender banner that spelled out the SPREE name. Rocco is a close personal friend of mine. He is also the leading film maker in the gay community.

Signs carried in the parade were slogans that we now see with increasing frequency. Here are some samples: "Homosexuality Is Natural Birth Control"; "More Deviation, Less Population"; "America: In God We Trust . . . Love It But Change It"; "Nazis Burned Jews, Churches Burned Homosexuals"; "Hickory, Dickory, Dock, They'll Pick Our Bedroom Lock, They'll Haul Us In and Call It Sin, Unless We Stop Their Clock."

We were the last in this smoothly run parade. I rode in an open convertible. Behind me came the congregation singing "Onward Christian Soldiers." We were gay, and we were proud. We had come out of our closets and into the streets. We were applauded—I think it was for our courage, and a kind of recognition for what we were doing in the religious community. It was a moving experience. I meditated because I had some misgivings about what lay immediately ahead. After the parade I went to the corner of Hollywood Boulevard and Las Palmas Avenue. I intended to begin a prayer-vigil and fast there. Prior to that, I had sent letters to Los Angeles Police Chief Davis and his administrative assistants to let them know my plans. I really didn't go there to be arrested. In the back of my mind there was always that chance that it could happen, but I really didn't think so. After all, the Krishna kids hadn't been arrested there. Neither had the Salvation Army people, nor any other religious group such as the gospel preachers and singers who have come out of Holiness churches and have gone there to preach, sing, solicit funds and demonstrate. No theater manager had ever been arrested for having people three deep along the boulevard waiting to buy tickets or waiting to be admitted to his theater.

So I chose a convenient spot and sat down. After I sat there about thirty minutes, some police officers walked up, looked the situation over, and one said, "Did you know that you're breaking the law?"

I looked up and said, "No I don't know that."

"It's against the law to do what you're doing," the other officer said.

"Well, if it's against the law to sit on the sidewalk, then I presume I'm breaking the law."

They then asked me to get up and move along. I said, "Well, officers, I can't do that. I'm holding a prayer-vigil and fast as a protest against the laws that discriminate against homosexuals here in the state of California." They left.

But they came back twice more with the same request, and I gave them the same answer. Meanwhile, some of my friends and supporters were marching up and down to show their support and approval of the prayer-vigil and fast. They read prayers, sang hymns, and walked in an orderly manner. A sergeant from the Los Angeles Police Department came up, looked at my clerical collar, and said, "Now, you're not going to be arrested, but I want you to know that you are in violation of the law." I thought I was going to be left alone.

It looked like I might be there awhile. Willie Smith had his VW bus parked around the corner. Steve was there with my mother, and a few others. Willie had brought jugs of water, air mattresses, and sleeping bags. He was all set to see that we would be as comfortable as possible. We settled in. Police cars would cruise slowly by, and I would see officers talking on their radios to headquarters. Then a fire truck went by, fairly close. My first thought was, God they're going to use water hoses to clear the people off the street. I told everyone who stood around to please leave at once. I told Steve to take Mother to Willie's bus. I told Willie that if anything happened, I didn't want him or Steve to be on the scene to get busted. They'd have to be free to function. He, reluctantly, went to his bus.

Two women sat down with me. They insisted on joining me for the prayer-vigil and the fast. They said they would stick it out to the end. Willie provided them with water, blankets, and air mattresses, too. One of the women was from the Daughters of Bilitis. The other was from an organization called HELP, Incorporated. DOB is a nonviolent, but militant organizaticn to aid lesbians in their fight for equal rights. HELP is the "Homophile Effort for Legal Protection."

Vigilant Morris Kight was there to help see that no violence occurred. Morris is a close personal friend of mine, one of my earliest supporters. He has been a civil rights activitist since World War II. Most of his action has centered on gay civil rights. Not only was he a founder of Gay Liberation Front, he has been a prime mover in all gay rights action for nearly two decades. Seeing Morris come forward to help see that everything ran smoothly bolstered my courage.

My secretary was walking along in the group of supporters, that was beginning to grow. I began to worry that the marching would stop and somebody would start something. My secretary was accompanied by two newspaper people, one was the then city editor of the *Hollywood Citizen News,* and the other was a charming and bright newspaperwoman from the same paper, who now writes for *The Los Angeles Times.* They were three abreast.

One police officer hailed my secretary, and I heard him shout to him, "Hey, you, come here!"

So, my secretary walked over, accompanied by his friends of the press, and he said, "Yes, officer?"

The officer said to them, "I'm talking to him. Who are you?" So they showed their press cards, and said they were covering this prayer-vigil and fast for the papers. The police officer's tone changed immediately. They asked him what he had to say. He replied, "You can only march two abreast!" So the city editor dropped behind.

When they passed me the next time, I stopped my secretary, and said, "I want you to get in the bus; I don't want you arrested. You'll have to be at the office to take care of the phones, the mail, and the general business. And I don't like the way things look around here. Try to have everyone keep moving, and not stop or bunch up. Pass that word as you leave." He did. And people began to leave and go away. The two girls and I talked about how smooth it all seemed to be going.

A police car rolled around the corner and stopped. Two policemen jumped out, came over and said, "You're all under arrest! Would you please come along peaceably and get into the car!" We stood up, walked over to the car, and got in the back seat. The doors were closed and locked. The officers got in the front. That made three of them up there. One radioed headquarters that they had picked us up, and that they hadn't had any trouble with any mob of any sort. One officer turned around and said, "If you promise not to try to jump out of the car, we won't handcuff you." By this time, we were really picking up speed on our way down the Boulevard.

"Don't worry. I won't try to jump out of this car or any that's doing sixty-five miles an hour. And neither will they. If anything should happen to us, people will know something went wrong, because we're not going to do anything violent. Period."

We were taken to the Hollywood police station at Wilcox Avenue, ushered up to the second floor and put into a room. We were there about ten minutes when a young police officer came in, sat down and began to talk to us. I think we discussed homosexuality with him for about three-quarters of an hour. He was most curious about us. He said that he'd never talked to homosexuals before, and he just didn't know what to think. This young man had been one of the arresting officers. A lieutenant from the force walked into the room, and said that we were going to be released on our O. R. (own recognizance).

I told him that I couldn't go along with that. I said, "No, I'm not going to be released."

He looked at me very suspiciously and asked, "Don't you want to get back down to Hollywood Boulevard?"

"No, I don't. I presume you would just arrest me again. I'll just stay here."

He smiled and said, "Why? Do you think this will get you some sort of publicity? Do you think that'll help your cause?"

"Well, I'll stay here. You've already picked me up on Hollywood Boulevard and you'd probably only arrest me again. So, I'll go ahead and spend the night in jail tonight. I won't sign myself out."

They immediately withdrew the offer, and that went for the girls, too. Both of them had to work the next day, so they had to start the procedure of raising bail. We were separated. I was taken downstairs, immediately fingerprinted, photographed, and booked. They were very courteous. By now it was well after midnight.

The jail was clean, and it had the jailhouse smell—kind of stale sulphur, I guess, or some kind of disinfectant, that seeps through everything. The floors were scrubbed clean, and the bars were painted green. I was given a mattress and taken to my cell. The turnkey told me to flop on whatever bunk I wanted. There were two steel frames that protruded from the wall. They were suspended by chains at each end. There was a toilet bowl attached to the wall at the other end. There is something about having that heavy steel door of bars clang shut behind you, and the lock flop over. Suddenly, I felt very much alone. I tossed my mattress onto the cot, and I stood and looked up. The light shone right back in my eyes. I closed my eyes and asked God to guide me through this. Then I straightened out the mattress, took off my coat, folded it, and laid it neatly on the cot. I folded my hands and prayed for a long time. Then I lay down, put my coat over my head to shut out the light and fell off to a light and troubled sleep. The sounds of the jail, loud voices, occasional curses, the belligerence of a drunk, traffic noises, sirens and sometimes someone crying, often awakened me. The emergency hospital was next door. The wailing siren and clanging bell sounds of an ambulance would crash into my brain. I would again say my prayers and doze off to sleep. Then I heard my own cell door open. I was getting a cellmate. He was a drunk. It was nearly four in the morning. The drunk took one look at my clerical collar, crossed himself and just stood there staring. I smiled, put my coat back over my head and fell back to sleep. The drunk just slumped down on the floor, huddled up and dozed. He snored so loudly that it was hard to fall back to sleep.

Then I heard a ruckus start in some other cell. I heard someone crying and screaming, "Don't, don't beat me." I jumped up. But I couldn't see anything. And then it was over. I could still hear the plaintive, whimpering sobs. My heart reached out to that poor soul. What had happened? I learned later that it was a young transvestite, determined to become a transsexual, who had been arrested for soliciting to perform a lewd act. This person had been thrown into a cell with other prisoners, and had been beaten up by them. The thing that was so horrible about it is that no one went to help him. The police just ignored him. It was the kind of indirect brutality that really galls me. They did nothing to him, but they refused to help him. Days later, I met the young person, and had a long heart-warming talk with him about his problems. Our church was able to help him in many ways: his court case, sexual orientation, job problems, but most important with friends.

I paced my cell, and prayed. I was offered breakfast, and I refused it because I was fasting. As soon as I refused that first meal, I was taken out of the cell and photographed again. I was taken to the front desk, and they put a new arm band on me. They took mine off, and I saw that the new one had the name of an individual I had never heard of. They also gave me a new booking number. That really scared me. I was sure that some strange game had started, and that I would be lost somewhere in the jail system of Los Angeles County or Los Angeles City, or traded back and forth.

"Say, this is a big mistake. This is the wrong name, and the wrong booking number."

They just laughed and said, "Oh, that's okay, don't worry, it doesn't make any difference."

No matter how much I protested, nothing penetrated their minds, nor their procedures. I was taken away and transferred immediately by car to the jail in the Highland Park-Lincoln Heights area. It is really a series of holding tanks with two jail divisions, fifty-eight and fifty-nine, for misdemeanor arraignments. The building was out on San Fernando Road, and it was fairly new. I was popped into a tank with about fifty other alleged criminals. One of them came up to me right away and said, "Father, what are you in for?"

I said, "I was nailed for being in a civil rights demonstration!" That did it. I was an instant hero. They crowded around me and shook hands. Most of them spoke Spanish. It's that kind of neighborhood out there. Some came and spoke to me in Spanish, and I regretted that I couldn't talk with them.

Finally, my case was called. I was led out and put in a small anteroom near the courtroom. I was approached by a public defender who asked if I had an attorney.

"No, not for today. I'll serve as my own attorney. But, when I go to trial, I'll have private counsel."

"You know that they're not going to let you out on your O. R. today? You should have taken that yesterday."

I just laughed and said, "Well, if they don't let me out, I'll just stay in jail, then, because I will not put up bail. And I'll just go on with my prayer-vigil and fast, while I'm in prison."

He looked me over and said, "I see." And he left.

About five minutes later, another attorney came in. He was a young Chicano. His attitude was the opposite of the voice of doom that had just left. He slapped me on the back and said, "Well, did you know that you made *The Los Angeles Times?* You're on the second page. And there's all kinds of press out there. The judge is hysterical. He wants to get you out of here as fast as he can."

That kind of bowled me over. "Well, the other public defender told me that I couldn't be released on my O. R., that I would have to be bailed out. And that I just plain refuse to do. I'll stay in prison to do my fasting, as part of my protest."

He laughed. "Don't worry, the judge won't ask you to bail yourself out. He's embarrassed by the whole situation, and he really wants you out of here—fast!"

So, I walked into the courtroom with this charming young man. When I appeared, about a half dozen people among the spectators stood up. A lot of others stood up, when they saw my collar, and some of them joined in this demonstration. Warmth flowed through me. I knew I wasn't lost or abandoned. I could see Steve, Mother, my secretary and several others. The judge did not stop the little ovation. He waited until it was quiet. Originally I had been told that I was to be charged with inciting to riot, but the charge had been reduced to simply obstructing a public sidewalk. The proceedings were short, sweet, cut, and dried. I pleaded not guilty to the charge, and asked to be released on my own recognizance. My Chicano attorney friend prompted me there. The judge set trial for July 9th and ordered my immediate release.

I didn't even have to go back through the whole waiting procedure to get my things. A bailiff just handed me an envelope and asked me to open it and sign for the contents. It held all of my effects. I signed, turned around, and as I put my things in my pockets, I walked out of the courtroom a free man—temporarily.

Then I got a closer look at those beaming faces. One was a young transvestite I knew. Here was this young man, still all done up in high drag. He'd been to an all night Gay Liberation dance. His mascara was running. He was crying. He needed a shave. His beard was coming through all of those layers of makeup. He was a sight. Well, the whole scene just bewildered everyone. Most didn't know what to make of it. We all embraced. We cried. We kissed on the cheek, and we hustled out of there.

What had gone on while I was jailed? That was something I wanted to know. How had they ever found me?

They'd practically sent out runners. My name had been purposely misspelled on the ledger at the Hollywood station, so I was apparently not there. No one knew, nor would anyone tell. When I'd been arrested, one officer kept saying, "Let's move along, quietly, we don't want another Watts here." Other officers joined him. But interest focused on the Hollywood station. I was inside, but no one could prove it. Rumors ran riot. Steve carried on. My mother cried. A bail bondsman finally found me. He persuaded everyone to go home, or to go on about their business. They did, but it was a sleepless, worrisome night all around.

The Gay Liberation Front was having a dance to celebrate Christopher Street West, the first anniversary of the gay riot in New York. That was the famous Stonewall riot when the New York police raided a gay bar, and the homosexuals fought back and said, "Enough. We're not going to be pushed any more." They made quite a stir, too. Ever since then a Gay Liberation Day is held throughout the country to celebrate Gay Pride Week. We have parades, dances and meetings; we put forth new efforts to stop police harassment and brutality; we try to change the antiquated and barbaric laws that are used almost exclusively against the homosexual community.

When news of the arrest reached the Gay Lib Dance over at Satan's Bar in the Silver Lake area, it did almost start a riot. Young people wanted to march on the police station. They probably would have, but they didn't know which one I was in. But Gay Lib founder, Morris Kight, who had made the announcement, called the crowd to order and assured it that I didn't want a march. I only wanted the fast to go on as scheduled. Arguments broke out as to how the people there would demonstrate their support for me. Morris told me that someone actually slapped him and tossed a glass of beer into his face. But, eventually, he was able to persuade them that the best thing would be a planned series of nonviolent demonstrations and marches downtown and in Hollywood to support the fast.

Morris, too, had spent a sleepless night. When he left the dance he went to my home to help my family take up its vigil of doubts and worries. They were all scared and anxious about just what was happening to me. Morris came with my family to the court proceedings and escorted me home from jail that morning, when we all came back home. I had to get cleaned up, and get some of the dry jailhouse clinging smell off me so I could breathe again. While I did that, they all made coffee and started to plan the next step. We discussed just what the arrest had done to the vigil. We talked over the parade, the vigil, the fast, and the arrest, of course. We agreed that I would not be making any progress by simply going back to Hollywood Boulevard. If I were arrested again it would simply defeat my purpose. I needed a new setting and a new means of attracting the attention of the people I had to reach, the ones in the establishment that really could be effective.

Morris agreed that I needed to dramatize the situation, but in some new area. He mentioned the First Unitarian Church, a congregation where young men avoiding military service were sometimes given sanctuary. The alternate location was the Federal Building in the heart of the Los Angeles civic center.

Before a decision was reached, Morris polled the group sitting somberly over their coffee cups. When he came to Mom she just broke down and started crying again. When Morris asked Steve, he said, "Wherever Troy wants to go, that's it."

Morris looked at me. "It's the Federal Building." I drew the new line of battle.

I took up my post on the steps of the Federal Building in downtown Los Angeles. I had a jug of water, an air mattress, a blanket, my Bible, and a Book of Common Prayer. I had to insist that my staff really stay on the job. That's where they were needed. There was a phone booth near me downtown, so if I was needed, I could be reached there. Supporters joined me. At least fifty from the church and others from other organizations wanted to come say prayers, sing hymns and maintain a vigil with me. How long would it take? I was often asked that question. I could only say that I would stay there until someone, somewhere in some arm of government, whether national, state, county, or local, came to say that they wanted to have a meaningful discussion, to say that they wanted to know about the unjust laws and the police and court abuse in the enforcement of these laws directed specifically at homosexuals. I wanted someone in the power structure to come and talk about what was wrong, and what could be done about it. I really didn't know how long I would be on those steps. But I was set for a long siege. About two hundred of my supporters a day came down and joined me whenever they could get off work, had any free time or could spend some hours in the late evening or early morning before going to work. At any one time I think anyone could have counted about three dozen people there. The two women who were arrested with me came and joined me, and just stayed right there. They had made tremendous sacrifices to do so.

Some asked why I had chosen the Federal Building. There, we were largely immune to harassment by the Los Angeles Police Department. The Federal Building had been the scene of many demonstrations in the past. One United States Marshal came out and told a reporter, "We don't expect to do anything about it. A man has the right to protest if he wishes, as long as it's in a peaceful manner." There were times when I would take a break to go home and clean up. I shower and shave at least once a day in such circumstances, and I conserve my energy and strength. I meditate and pray. I talk and pray with passersby, and with those who are with us. Time passes. But waiting for some sign that God has moved the adversary is sometimes very trying. When I feel that way, I know that He is just testing me again.

Two of my supporters had gone back to the corner of Las Palmas and Hollywood Boulevard and slept the night there totally unmolested. They brought their sleeping bags and were largely ignored by the police.

The fourth full day of the fast, I had a call from television station KHJ-TV, Channel 9, in Los Angeles. They had a program called "Tempo." I was to be interviewed on the air on that program in the morning. The interview was arranged by my secretary and by Bob Grant, who would do the interview, and by the station management. There was a telephone tie-in that went through our parsonage office and to the phone booth near me on the Federal Building steps. The connection was made. It seems to me it was around noon. Someone brought along a portable tv set so we could watch, and hear. And the connection worked. I heard Mr. Grant say, "I am now going to talk to a minister, Reverend Troy D. Perry. He was the prime mover and leader of the Homosexual Parade this last week on Hollywood Boulevard. He was arrested for blocking the sidewalk and is now in his fourth or fifth day of fasting at the Federal Building. Now, I believe that I have him on the line. First of all, I just can't bring myself to call you Reverend Perry, so I'll just call you Mr. Perry. So, Mr. Perry . . ." He was interrupted by a loud click. I hung up. This was the kind of put down that was long behind us. We watched on the television and he tried to revive the interview.

His partner said, "I think he hung up."

The loudest dial tone I've ever heard came through the television speaker.

Later, I learned that the result of my hanging up had had an electrifying response. My secretary called the station and demanded an apology. He insisted that a reporter should be objective. When he lost his objectivity, he was no longer either a reporter or a good editor. If the apology was not made publicly on the air, the station would be picketed by all the gay organizations that supported me. That got action. A campaign to call and write the station started. Once started, it didn't stop. The next day I got the apology, and it was widely covered in the press. The following week Regis

Philbin took over. Where Grant is now, I don't know, but "Tempo" goes on. I've appeared on it, both in person and by phone, many, many times. I regret Grant's demise. His apology was most sincere. I think he learned a great lesson from it. No matter what his personal feelings are, he knows the ethics of his profession. I hope he is prospering in it.

But we had just begun. It was only June 29th. People came and went. My prayer-vigil and fast went on. Nothing seemed to be happening, but on July 2nd, I received a visit from a man we had supported in a special election of the preceding year. We had helped him, and we had defeated his opponent. He was City Councilman Robert J. Stevenson. His district included Hollywood. He and Mrs. Stevenson came to again express their friendship and their thanks for my support. Councilman Stevenson was to become a real ally of ours. Some time later, he was arrested by the Los Angeles Police Department Vice Squad, and charged with attempting to give a bribe in a gambling scandal in downtown Los Angeles. He fought this case through to an acquittal, but it alerted him to the built-in immunity that the police department has from civilian review. It was he who uncovered the fact that the Los Angeles Vice Squad has, in its budget, over six million dollars to fight victimless crimes of vice.

But at that time he presented me with a letter, a written statement asking me to reconsider my decision to remain on a hunger strike in these times. "Martyrs are soon forgotten. The work to which you have dedicated yourself may be lost without your guidance."

He further urged me as follows: "You can better serve your cause by pressing for legal reform in Sacramento, and make no mistake about it, it cannot be done at any local legislative level. I urge you, Reverend Perry, not to become a political dropout, but rather to continue your efforts at the proper legislative level . . . ." The letter went on, but that was the main point.

I thanked Councilman Stevenson, and told him that I appreciated his concern for my health, "But I don't feel, at this point, that I can stop my fast. I certainly don't feel I will be a political dropout in my struggle to get these laws changed. While the legislature does not meet in the Los Angeles area, I do feel that there is something that city officers can do. City councilmen could publicly express their views on pending legislation that is now bottled up in Sacramento in a legislative committee."

I referred to Assembly Bill Number 437, introduced by Assemblyman Willy Brown of San Francisco. This bill, defeated several times previously, would legalize sex acts in private between consenting adults. At that time, the bill was stalled in the Criminal Procedures Committee by Chairman Frank Murphy, Jr., Republican of Santa Cruz.

At my prayer-vigil and fast I passed out leaflets, as did everyone with me. By the time I had received Councilman Stevenson's letter, I had personally passed out over five thousand leaflets. These leaflets urged everyone to phone, telegraph, write, or go and see his assemblyman and senator to get the so-called Brown Bill out of committee, and to a vote, and then to vote for it. We pleaded with people to bring the matter to the attention of their legislators.

We didn't expect any problems from the Los Angeles Police Department. They wouldn't come unless the federal marshals called them, and they didn't. But, when they passed us on their way down the street to police headquarters, they often made obscene gestures, shouted some obscene phrases, or hit the brakes on the squad cars and touched the siren. It made a rather humorous, vulgar, and disconcerting sound.

After ten days of my prayer-vigil and fast, I didn't know how long I could really hold out, but my fast ended that day. Three city councilmen came and visited me. They wanted a list of grievances on police harassment, police brutality, unfair law enforcement, and discriminatory practices on the local level. They also promised to push for law reform through the legislature. They wanted to enter into a continuing and meaningful dialogue with us that would achieve positive results. For me, it was a personal victory. But more important, it was a victory for the whole gay community. I felt that it was fulfilling God's mission, but I knew my work had only just hit its stride.

Ahead lay growing pains, a search for a permanent home, and the real campaign to change attitudes on discrimination. There was also a little matter of the case I had pending against me in the criminal courts for maliciously obstructing the sidewalk.

Chapter Eight
Growing Pains

In opening a dialogue with the establishment, local, state, and federal officials, I felt that we were building understanding with the straight, or heterosexual, community. What most of us have found, especially on an individual level, is that a great deal of what is believed to be prejudice is in reality a facade: there's a lot of live and let live. There's a lot of accommodation. There's a lot of guilt there for the traditional feeling of oppression, and there is also a very hard core of fear, prejudice, and oppression, mostly represented by the personal prejudices of many key law enforcers. Our task has been to enlighten all, but to especially try to pry open the closed minds of those who would rather be blind to the human needs of the homosexual than to follow the real principles of Christ.

We have won some skirmishes in our battle against ignorance and prejudice, but the major battles still lie ahead. We will have to effect a basic change in laws governing sexual matters between consenting adults; what I do in my bedroom is no one's business but mine and my partner's, as long as we're both adults. I'm not passive. What I do, I like to do, and I think everyone should have that same choice. But I am opposed to sexual conduct when force is used on another person, or when it is destructive, either sadistically or masochistically. I think the sexual activity that people indulge in should be mutually adoring, respectful, and satisfying. That comes about through love and affection, along with education and enlightenment. That way one can learn to accept himself, to accept others, and to make an accommodation with society.

One of the reasons I'm drawn to younger people is that I like their attitude. Most of them are free, not uptight, nor put off by what anyone does sexually. They are the hope of the future in fighting all forms of bigotry, prejudice, and oppression. With the revolution in educational methods that is now taking place, it seems that the body of prejudice against us may be thought out, and the old attitudes challenged by young people.

This is the basic reason that so many young people have been drawn into our church. They have their own club, their own choirs, and they have even conducted entire church services on Sunday. They are true crusaders who take to the pulpits and to the street demonstrations with me to fight for our crusade.

Sometimes that crusade seems endless. It seems as if I'm playing the same record over and over. My court case is a primary example. My case came to trial on August 12, 1970. My attorney insisted that it was a civil liberties case; Judge James Harvey Brown insisted that it was not. Homosexuality was mentioned in the defense. Bella Stumbo and Morris Kight testified that I had had no malicious intent in going to Hollywood Boulevard and Las Palmas to begin my prayer-vigil and fast. I testified that I had made every effort to avoid blockage of the sidewalk by anyone, my supporters or the curious. I had tried to keep the crowd, small though it was, moving in an orderly fashion.

Nevertheless, I was convicted. My sentence was a suspended jail term of ninety days in the county jail, and a fine of fifty dollars, plus summary probation for one year. We decided immediately to appeal the case.

While I waited for the appeal, I went on with my church duties. My supporters joined me in a program staged by Willie Smith at the Troupers Hall on North La Brea near Hollywood Boulevard. Over three hundred turned out to donate funds at the benefit show to raise money for me to make the appeal. Justice still has a price tag in this country. Appeals cost a lot of money, and so do legal services.

Meanwhile, I felt that however humiliating it might be for my colleagues, I would ask them to join me in the very activist part of our crusade. The generation gap closed; people of all ages came forward. Some were not able to help without placing their livelihood in danger, but we gained a great deal of strength. We were more deeply involved as a new denomination, a legal entity. We became the Universal Fellowship of Metropolitan Community Churches. Our missions and congregations rushed to join. San Diego stole a march, even on Los Angeles, the Mother Church. It was first to join the Fellowship, Los Angeles second.

There were those who worked very hard in the church, but who wanted us all to go slow, to take a very conservative posture in our approach to any social reforms. They felt, in all honesty, that political action, demonstrations, fasts, and marches were premature. I didn't agree then; I still don't. But I respect their opinions. They made their voices heard in board of directors meetings and in meetings of our parishes and in the congregation. I felt that the spectrum of the church's outreach was such that it would accommodate all. It does! No one got mad and walked out because I had taken to the streets or the steps of the Federal Building. I had to clear the air after the fast because that had brought matters to a head in my own church.

As a result of our meeting, we went ahead and decided to expand. We would open new missions; we would carry the word of God, but we would do anything we could legally do, provided it was *nonviolent,* to aid the plight of homosexuals everywhere. Avoiding involvement would limit our church and tend to make it somewhat sterile, the very image we were trying to avoid.

Some thought that we were too closely following or aping the other established churches. This was reflected in the performances of marriages, the blessing of homosexual unions.

We decided to simply reject the restricting and artificial moral codes that we felt were petrifying society. If couples wished to strengthen and formalize their unions, what should prevent them? Nothing! We felt, too, that such unions would strengthen our hand in showing how silly some laws that rigidly guide sexual and moral conduct really are, especially in California.

Our ceremony is revolutionary when you consider it in traditional religious or legal concepts. Actually, there has been a series of historical precedents that even predate Christianity in having marriages between couples of the same sex. It was not a worldwide practice in ancient times, but there is evidence of the marriages in various cultures, both ancient and primitive, in the Orient, Africa, the Near East, and around the Mediterranean. I feel that our ceremony blessing such a union is a demand for the re-evaluation of sexual ethics. Most couples we married were those who had been together for years. They found that formalizing or solemnizing their relationship simply strengthened the bond that they had already developed. It added a new dimension.

In our discussions of gay marriages, we decided that we would broaden the basis for people to live together. Formerly, love was thought to exist only between people of the opposite sex. Then love was regarded as an ideal state if the couple was considering having a family. This developed into a union that was considered a complete state, even without children. Finally, we determined that it should simply be the loving relationship between any two people, and that this was just as valid and should be sanctioned.

Most churches have not considered the homosexual, and certainly not a gay couple. They wouldn't consider a gay marriage at all, primarily because it doesn't produce families. The fact that marriage is traditionally an institution to produce offspring is an early basis for marriage. If it were the only basis upon which gay people are denied the rite of marriage, then by the same token marriage should be denied to a great number of heterosexual couples who either cannot or will not have children. Personally I feel that if this logic is carried through to a conclusion, then after a certain specified period of time has elapsed without progeny, the marriage should automatically be declared dissolved.

As years have passed many marriage laws have changed. The attitude about marriage is much more relaxed. Now Jews and Christians may legally intermarry in most cultures. Formerly such a union was a capital crime. Races are often forbidden intermarriage. Only recently in this country have the legal bans against interracial marriages been stricken. But the prejudice against them goes on. In Metropolitan Community Church we have a ritual that we feel is only one more step in the direction of making all marriage rites more realistic and much closer to actual situations. We do screen couples who want a religious ceremony. I think we're much more thorough in our preceremonial counseling than many churches.

We insist that the couple has a close ongoing relationship for at least six months. We counsel them about special problems, promiscuity, and how to cooperate in establishing a fulfilling and meaningful relationship.

Most people we have married are still together. We advise them to go slow, not to rush, be easy with each other. Usually, the move into the wedded state has been more cautious than in the heterosexual world. Incidentally, church membership is not required.

Everyone wants to know whether such marriages are legal under California law. As of now, they are: Section 4213 of the State Code states than when two persons, not minors, have been living together, as an espoused couple, they may be married by any clergyman. A certificate made by the clergyman, entered on his church records, and delivered to the couple is sufficient. No other record need be made.

One couple did have the marriage recorded at the county clerk's office, and another couple received a letter stating that it was not necessary to have it recorded, that the marriage was quite legal if performed by a clergyman.

At this time we were also having a controversy over what constituted pastoral duties. Did my duties cease when I was involved in homosexual rights demonstrations outside the church? Since my involvement is total, it cannot be otherwise than what I am now making it. My pastoral duties are all-inclusive and extend into all areas at all times. But I was able to take a short vacation in 1970. I am entitled to one month a year, at my discretion.

On January 28, 1971, I got some really good news. The appellate court had reversed the judgment against me in my misdemeanor conviction for maliciously obstructing the sidewalk. The case was remanded for a new trial.

The Memorandum Opinion is interesting:

PEOPLE OF THE STATE OF CALIFORNIA 71-45
Plaintiff and Respondent,

vs.

TROY D. PERRY,
Trial Court No. 364356
Defendant and Appellant.   CR.   A.   *9777*
January 28, 1971
Appeal by defendant from judgment of the Municipal Court of the Los Angeles Judicial District, James Harvey Brown, Judge.

Judgment reversed; cause remanded for new trial.

MEMORANDUM OPINION

On this appeal from his conviction of blocking a public sidewalk in violation of section 647c of the Penal Code, defendant complains of evidentiary rulings which he contends prevented him from presenting a defense of discriminatory enforcement. After leading a parade on Hollywood Boulevard, defendant sat on the sidewalk under circumstances which the trial court found constituted a violation of section 647c. The parade apparently was a protest, at least in part, by homosexuals, and defendant, who is a minister, sat down on the sidewalk assertedly to conduct a prayer vigil in support of pending legislation on the subject of sex activities between consenting adults. During cross-examination of a witness for the prosecution, a police officer, defense counsel asked him about the sidewalk activities of a particular religious group. The prosecution's objection of the ground of irrelevancy was sustained. Although defense counsel indicated his purpose was to show discriminatory enforcement, the court ruled that "the introduction of evidence with respect to some other group is not relevant." Counsel stated he would defer to the ruling. Similarly, after defendant testified on direct examination that the parade permit had not been readily granted, his attorney asked him, "What did you have to do to get it." The People objected, and, in response to defense counsel's reference to discriminatory enforcement, the trial court stated, "That's not an issue here," and ruled, "the testimony in that respect is . . . immaterial and irrelevant."

The foregoing rulings were error. Discriminatory enforcement is a valid defense to prosecution under a criminal statute. [*Cox* vs. *Louisiana* (1965) 379 U.S. 357 (13 Law Ed. 541, 85 S.Ct. 441); *People* vs. *Gray* (1967)

254 Cal. App. 2d 256 (63 Cal Rptr. 211, ; *People* vs. *Haag,*
Cr. A. 8985.] The People seek to support the trial
court's rulings on the ground that discriminatory enforcement was not an issue in the case. They argue that
defendant was not prepared to present evidence of discriminatory enforcement and "was engaging in a per-
functory fishing expedition." While not clearly
articulated, the argument appears to be that the defendant cannot properly claim error in the rulings exclud-
ing evidence or prejudice therefrom because he made
no offer of proof. The argument cannot be supported.
Defendant was entitled to proved discriminatory enforcement, if he could, by cross-examination of the
People's witness. *People* vs. *Gray* points out that, "Evidence of discriminatory enforcement usually lies bur-
ied in the consciences and files of the law enforcement
agencies involved and must be ferreted out by the defendant." (*Supra*, at p. 266.) And, as stated in *Tossman*
vs. *Newman* (1951) 37 Cal. 2d 522, 525 (233 P.2d 1),
"Questions on cross-examination . . . are largely ex-
ploratory, and it is unreasonable to require an offer of
proof since counsel cannot know what pertinent facts
may be elicited. Hence no offer of proof is necessary in
order to obtain a review of rulings on cross-examination." (See Evidence Code #354c.) With respect to the
question put to defendant on direct examination to
which objection was sustained, it is clear from the
record that it was preliminary to a showing of police
opposition to the parade permit. Since the trial court
clearly indicated or intimated that it would receive no
evidence on the issue of discriminatory enforcement,
"an offer of proof is not a prerequisite to arguing on
appeal the prejudicial nature of the exclusion of such
evidence." [*Lawless* vs. *Calaway* (1944) 24 Cal. 2d 81
(147 P.2d 604).] Moreover, an offer of proof is dis-
pensed with where the "substance, purpose and rele-
vance of the excluded evidence was made known to the

trial court by the questions asked ... or by other means." (Evidence Code #354a.)

There was evidence in the record which negated discriminatory enforcement and defendant may have been unprepared to present any evidence in support of his claim. Nevertheless, as stated in *Lawless* vs. *Calaway, supra,* at p. 92, "While it may be true that favorable answers to the questions propounded would not have supplied the deficiency of proof in this case, (defendant) was precluded from continuing with the examination of the witness and developing further the line of inquiry which might have elicited the essential" proof, and "the questions to which objections were sustained were appropriate preliminaries to a more complete examination, and prejudice ensued from the cutting off *in limine* of all inquiry on a subject with respect to which (defendant) was entitled to examine" the witnesses. The judgment is reversed; cause is remanded for new trial.

KATZ, Judge

We concur: WHYTE, Presiding Judge

ZACK, Judge

The second trial took place on April 28, 1971. It was recessed after the prosecution phase was presented. The trial resumed on May 11th. In making the recess Judge Joseph R. Grillo stated that he thought I was guilty.

My defense centered on discriminatory enforcement. We were not able to get Chief Edward M. Davis of the Los Angeles Police Department to testify. My sentence in the second trial was the same as the first trial. I had again insisted that I had attempted to keep the sidewalks open to all pedestrian traffic, that I had gone there with absolutely no malicious intent and that I was entitled to the same treatment that other religious organizations get when they use sidewalks to further their own ends. We insisted that I was not responsible for the actions of onlookers. The case has again been appealed, and is proceeding through the courts. It will probably finally end up before the United States Supreme Court, if nothing else happens to close the case.

From the first few weeks I knew that Metropolitan Community Church would reach other communities, other states, and, sooner or later, other nations. I had no idea that it would grow with the speed it did. It seems to me, now, that it must have been a matter of timing, and I think that it was fate, too! God chose me for my mission at a time when He knew the world would respond, once the need was made clear.

People came to visit us from other California cities, and from Arizona, from Texas, from Illinois, from Hawaii, from Canada, from just about everywhere. They wanted to find out how to start MCC in their communities. We had a program set up to help others start a mission. We also had visiting clergymen who traveled to various places to help get services going. Very important, we had a number of clergymen who were like Reverend Richard Ploen and Papa John Hose. They came forward and said, "Here we are, we're gay, and we want to help." They came and stayed at the mother church in Los Angeles, acquainted themselves with our administrative procedures, with our social and political action programs; they also got to know the people who are so actively furthering our cause in Los Angeles.

Thus equipped, they went back to their communities, or sometimes to new ones, and started out. We don't have any real failures yet. We have had some false starts, or some discouraging starts, where we had to begin anew because facilities didn't develop, pledges weren't met on time, or personnel just couldn't match their performance with their enthusiasm at that time. But we continue to grow. We now have nearly three thousand members scattered around this great country of ours, and we have thousands more that we reach through our efforts!

No matter how rapidly we expanded, we were never able to catch up with all that we needed in the way of housing

and our services to the gay community. We needed a permanent church home. Finally, in late 1970 we found one. We
looked over an old church in downtown Los Angeles. Part
of it had been built in 1906; a larger addition was built in
1916. Architecturally it was what is called Akron, after the
city in Ohio, not the chain store in California. The church
was in a rundown neighborhood, and it was almost hope-
lessly a wreck. But it was centrally located, and it was big.
We envisioned fixing it over to meet our needs.

The building was part of an estate. We had trouble clearing the title because two heirs were minors, but the matter
was taken up, and we bought the building. We then spent
a fortune remodeling it. Where would we get the money? I
was determined, even before we could think of moving into
our own church, to get a really solid building fund going.

In the early days of my church, when we were having our
own population explosion, I asked almost everyone to contribute to a special building fund for that day when we could
buy or build our own church home. I knew we'd make it.
The fund grew slowly, far too slowly. I am not a patient
man. Things have just got to move. So one Sunday I
preached, and challenged the congregation to raise ten thousand dollars in one week's time. I wanted to see it there by
next Sunday. I could see in a few a feeling of utter disbelief.
That gave way to a rather confident feeling. They knew
along with me, that I had no doubts that God would provide.

Sunday, October 19, 1969 filled me with a tingling excite-
ment. I had to know not *if* my prayers were answered, but
how. My heart swelled as I went in and heard people say that
they were sure we would raise the money. Strangely, no one
said exactly what he personally would do to see that our
building fund campaign went over the top. Yet everyone to
me seemed convinced that we'd have the money. I never
heard anyone say, "Well, I'll give ten or twenty or maybe
more." The atmosphere was calm, quiet, and rather reverent.

During the preceding week I had some inkling of what
was in the wind. One person donated his residual check;

another the money he would have spent on his Halloween drag costume; another donated a gift. These donations had trickled in all week. I preached about building a house of prayer as a fitting tribute to the Lord. With that I told them that I had prayed and fasted during the week. So great was my faith in God and the congregation that I had brought a twenty-gallon trash can to collect the money for our church home. I placed the can in what I called "deep water," down in front of the first row of seats. I explained that the collection plates would never hold enough.

We would all march by and give what we could. We would march row by row and give. I asked if someone could play that old-time hymn, "Give Me That Old Time Religion." Someone rushed to the organ and started it out. Willie Smith stepped up and in his own Aimee Semple McPherson style, took the microphone and led the congregation in verse after verse. It ignited the whole group. Hands clapped. Feet stomped. The faithful marched. They came by emptying pockets, paper bags and coffee cans, and tossing checks, bills and coins into that trash can. The ushers did a great job of keeping everything moving so that no one got all tangled up in the rush of traffic. So it went row after row. The lyrics of the old hymn rose and died. Someone changed it to "if it's good enough for MCC, it's good enough for me." People waved, hooted, stamped, shouted, and cried like babies. I'd never seen so many wet-eyed faces pass in front of me. When the last row had passed, and it looked as if we could settle down, I heard someone call out, "Pass the plates!" I could hardly believe it, but I sure got those plates into the ushers' hands in a hurry. Even with those empty pockets in the crowd, there was the clink of coins and the rustling of bills. When that ended, and I thought we could get on with the services, two fellows from down in front jumped up and said, "We've marched for everything else, why not march for Jesus?" It electrified everyone. They just jumped up and marched up and down the aisles singing that same hymn. I never expected this from a group that is not just out and out

Pentecostal. The choir added to the zeal by clapping in double time. The emotion of religious ecstasy finally spent itself. We had a long line for communion. Everyone seemed to feel the spirit of abundance that filled the air. The church treasurer and his helpers went upstairs and counted the money during the last part of the service. We waited. It seemed like it would never come to us, that suspenseful moment of truth. I had a lump in my throat. Someone handed me a slip of paper. I knew what it was, but I wasn't sure I'd be able to speak. I puzzled a moment over the message. It said, "The count isn't complete. The change hasn't been counted, but we are a little over the ten thousand dollar mark already."

I looked out over the congregation, a sea of faces lost in the lights that illuminated the altar. The light didn't blind me. Tears did. There was a long, awesome silence.

Someone jumped up and yelled, "THA-N-K Y-O-U-U, J-E-E—Z-U- S!!!" The whole place seemed to explode, come apart, and settle back down. Wave after wave of applause 'shook the Encore to its foundations. The organist started playing "Praise God From Whom All Blessings Flow," and everyone joined in. We were late, and to the strains of that solemn hymn we filed out of the theater. But everyone seemed to want to prolong that moment. It passed almost too quickly, but I felt my determination even more firmly welling up in me. Now I knew we could not be stopped.

In less than a year we repeated the whole scene one more time, but we still didn't have enough. We knew where we wanted to go. There was a building available at bargain basement rates, but could we get it while it was still on the market? We knuckled down and explored every resource. We were still short. Finally Papa John, who was holding a resources ways and means committee meeting asked one of the deacons who luckily had wealthy parents if they might lend us the money. A long distance call was placed, our plight explained, and the charming woman on the other end said, "What did you expect us to do?" Papa John said, "We rather hoped that you'd be in a position to lend us the money." There was a hasty conference on the other end, and both people got on to assure us the money was on the way. This was converted into a donation, and a strange coincidence took place. About that same amount was returned to that couple as a tax refund.

Finally we had the money to go ahead. We raced.

It was almost two years and one week since the church had had its first services. Now we were closing escrow for a church home. We wanted to move in the last of February, so we had volunteers as well as the contractors come down to the church. Some worked right around the clock, worked until they almost dropped. First, we had a gigantic clean up to get some of the debris stacked as tall as a man in the main sanctuary of the building. We had to have door locks put on so we could go there and work and keep away the drunks who used the building to flop in, or for toilet facilities.

What did it need? Everything: new roofing, stucco for the walls, new windows, plastering, painting, wood paneling, floor finishing, carpeting, additional plumbing, installation of a kitchen in the basement, remodeling of some rooms, combining some and expanding others—it was a major job. It took us around three months to have the building ready for occupancy, or ready enough to start using it—and use it we did!

Chapter Nine
Home!

In late February, 1971, over a thousand people all over this nation got an engraved invitation in their morning mail:

You are cordially invited to attend
the Dedication of the Metropolitan
Community Church, The Mother Church
at 2201 South Union Avenue,
Los Angeles, California 90007
on Sunday, March 7, 1971, at 11:00 a.m.

R. S. V. P.   *Rev. Troy D. Perry,*   *Pastor and Founder*

The day had finally arrived. Our growing pains were still physically evident everywhere. The church building we occupied was indeed a large structure. We had completely remodeled. I forced the issue of moving in when we did because we so desperately needed the space and the facilities. "We'll have to build it around us while we work. We're one week late in dedication, but we can't make another postponement," I insisted to the contractors and to the hundreds of the congregation who worked around the clock to make the dream come true.

And there I stood, at last, in my black robe, my white cassock, and totally surrounded by an envelope of sound and music as the second hand ticked toward that magical hour of eleven, when we'd march in our first formal procession into our first religious service in the building that we now owned and called our home, the building we came to consecrate and dedicate that Sunday morning, March 7, 1971. Let me share with you my feelings of the dedication.

My colleagues and my family crowded around me, but the jam of people and the sounds of whispered voices, hushed conversations, organ and instrumental music, the multitude singing a hymn of praise to God, swirled around me. In less than two and one-half years, we had come so far.

As I reflect upon this, I am again back in the church that Sunday morning.

I hear Willie Smith bidding everyone welcome to Metropolitan Community Church of Los Angeles. Usually he leads the "Singspiration" before services. It is a real revivalist type warm-up. But today it is different. Today he is to sing a solo, "The Impossible Dream," from *Man of La Mancha.*

Willie dedicates the song to me, and I hear the applause, and I am embarrassed. Why me? I hear murmurs of approval and "Amens" and another round of applause as everyone seems to become united with Willie in this dedication. It is heartwarming. The feeling being generated reaches out and envelopes all of us. I no longer feel alone. I feel one with these people, and one with God.

As the introduction to the song plays, Willie says, "This isn't a hymn ordinarily sung in churches. But it is fitting for us. And it is fitting today. I've known Reverend Perry for a number of years. When he first told me that he was going to start this kind of church—this church—I thought he'd flipped out. And I told him he was crazy. You'll never get a bunch of queens to go along with it. But if you really are that crazy, I'll not only go along with you, I'll back you one hundred percent—all the way—in any way that I can. So, here we are less than three years later, in our own church home. The quest, the dream, is a reality." Willie has stood with us all the way.

The words of "The Impossible Dream" pour forth. Willie is really in excellent voice today. He's been practicing for this occasion, and he doesn't have any Sunday morning huskiness. As I feel moved by the lyrics and the melody of this great song, I think how right it is for all of us. To pursue this quest for self, a quest for self-respect, a quest for spiritual fulfillment, we have had to move to a new land, a promised land in our own minds. We have had to realize that too much has happened to us; we can never go back. We are all truly involved in a crusading mission in life, as rigorous in its way as was the Mormon trek westward, as permanent and as indomitable. For us, life will never be the same. We must continue in our quest for the spiritual fulfillment that we are finding here. Today, now, we are in our own church. And today, here, we are exalting in dedicating this building to God.

The lyrics of "The Impossible Dream" are so right for us. That's really what our task was, what it seemed. I have often heard others say the same, but we made it a possible dream for us. I don't really know how. We just did it. We're like the bumble bee that isn't supposed to be able to fly, if it follows the physical laws of flight. The bumble bee doesn't know that, of course, so it goes ahead and flies anyway. That's what we did. So many of us held on and fought this thing through. In our first year, we had five homes, some as temporary as two weeks, all impermanent. Part of our dream was this church. Impossible? Yes, but it is only our base of operations, a place from which we work, a place from which we reach out.

The song ends. Bill Thorne, our chairman of deacons, reads the Epistle. All about, I sense the appreciation that our first service in our new church home is really under way. I bow my head in a short silent prayer. The Epistle ends; the processional starts. Steve bears the banner of our church. Our national and state flags are carried in and positioned. The choir enters, with which an instrumental ensemble, with organ and piano, have presented the "Entrata Festivo." It is stirring and traditional, this solemn march. I have a sense of eternity, of oneness with the universe as I slowly march down the center aisle amid this throng turned out in their Sunday best. Everyone of them stands. Here and there a familiar face, many such faces, as I walk along. They recede into a blur as the perspective changes. We mount the steps to the altar. We pause at the altar, pray, and bow our heads in reverence and respect. Now, the ministers, the elders and I proceed to the right side of the altar, to our chairs. We remain standing. Reverend Richard Ploen goes to the podium to deliver the opening prayer.

As I bow my head, I see that the sunlight streaming in through the great stained-glass windows and the interior lighting make the church glow with a golden hue. Strangely, on the green rug in front of the altar, the altar's golden cross is reflected. It is diffuse, but it is rather startling. I feel uplifted, solemnized by prayer.

We remain standing for one of our favorite hymns, "He Lives." Today we have a new printed program, as extensive as one you might read for opera house performances. In it, we have printed the words of all of today's hymns, prayers, and rites of dedication. As we turn to the proper page in the program, or in the hymnals, I recall what a time we had raising enough money to buy hymnals.

"He Lives" catches everyone. It's that kind of hymn. People who come to church a few times catch themselves humming it. The tune runs through the mind, and it won't let go. I think the words are more meaningful to us. Christ does live within our hearts.

The informal portion of our service is the welcome by Papa John Hose. Various announcements are being given. We begin to get better acquainted. We all always shake hands with those sitting near us, and bid them welcome, and say, "God Bless You." Somehow, this makes everything more of an earthy, human, as well as religious experience.

More hymns, the Gospel and the always exciting "Gloria." We enter to more devout parts of our service with a prayer hymn. Today it is "Eternal Father, Strong to Save," and then we shall have the silent and the pastoral prayer. This again, as always, is prayed by Reverend Ploen. We remember those who are ill, those with problems, those who want special prayers, those bereaved, and those who have despaired.

Pat Rocco, a personal friend of mine, makes his own moving and personal contribution by a most reverent singing of "The Lord's Prayer."

I go forward, changing the mood. Sometimes I think it's a little bit of a shame to break up such a pleasant and prayerful meditation. But I feel so full of energy, and I love these people so much. I respond to them, as they do to me. We charge each other's batteries, and give each other energy and the strength and courage to go on.

It's incredible to see all of these people, many standing against the walls. We have all joined together for the greater glory of God, but we must do so in all humility. They go together. Without both we would lose sight of our true mission in life.

As I stride to the pulpit, I feel the congregation reaching out toward me, as I reach out to them—to each one of them. It is a spiritual handclasp. I feel sure of myself, but I know that it comes from the inspiration that God gives me. It warms me so. And that warmth fills the room. It always does.

"If you love the Lord this morning, would you say, amen!"

Everybody does shout, "Amen." I am replenished by the

roar of "amens" resounding through me. I stand there for a moment. I love these people so much. They inspire me every time I go before them. I know that some of them think I'm a cornball. Some think my accent makes me sound like a kind of Bible Belt hellfire and damnation preacher on the old Chatauqua circuit. The Pentecostal church is a shouting, praying, God-fearing denomination, and I'm surely the "Pecks' Bad Boy" of that sect. But that sect has influenced my church, probably as much as it has my whole life, every element of it.

"I want to apologize to some of you. You know I said, even just a week ago, that some of you had to stand up. And that when we got to our new church home, you wouldn't have to do that, anymore. I apologize for fibbing. We must have about three hundred people standing around the walls, up in the balcony and all over. And we praise the Lord for that today. Isn't it good to be home?"

A chorus of "amens" rolls back at me. It fills the church. There is such joy.

"Well, all right!"

More "amens." Then a wave of applause starts out there somewhere. It is picked up by everyone and rocks this church building. It has to be God's will and His blessings. It is a large building with seating for over eight hundred. It is such a beautiful day. I look at all these beautiful people. It is rapture.

"God bless you! This has been a long time coming. And you just don't know! But a lot of people do now, I think, know—really know—the struggle we have had, but we've made it."

"Amens" pour out and sprinkle my talks and my sermons rather like salt.

"We've waited for this day. We've looked for this day. And there are all kinds of people. Some of them are listed on the program for some of their donations, and I'd like to thank all of them right now. Some are listed in the church bulletin. Some are not. Many, many came and gave of their time and energies. They are young men, young women, old men, old women, who were down here from sunrise to sunset, and 'til one and two o'clock in the morning—especially during these last three weeks, getting this place ready. And we're still not ready.

"We don't have our permanent chairs in yet. These are with the compliments of Abbey Rents, or compliments of the board of directors I should say. Through Abbey Rents. We went ahead and rented the chairs so we could worship today. We can praise the Lord that we have a roof over our heads that we can call home. And I can think of people, and I could start calling out their names this morning. But I won't start. I just want to give you all the opportunity to give a great big hand. Maybe this is uncouth in church, but do let's hear it! Let's give a great big round of applause to all the people who were down here working so hard. All right—now!"

The wave of applause is deafening. I have to sneak a look at those beautiful leaded stain glass windows, and hope that they'll stay in. These rounds of deafening applause soar around this church. I can really feel the vibrations. Everyone who has worked here for so long and so hard must glow inwardly because there is this deeply felt appreciation of all that has gone on.

"Now we have all kinds of visitors from gay organizations here in Los Angeles as well as from all over the country. Just a few who are with us this morning are representatives from the Daughters of Bilitis; the Gay Liberation Front; the Mattachine Society; One, Incorporated; the Society for Individual Rights (usually known only as SIR) headquartered up in San Francisco.

"We are honored to have delegations from our various missions and congregations around the country that could make it to be here with us today. Please keep it down to a mild roar as you acknowledge the following: Costa Mesa, San Diego, Phoenix, Oakland, and San Francisco.

"It's a pleasure to introduce the founder of the Church of One Brotherhood, one of the first 'gay' churches in America.

"We have some letters and telegrams, and all kinds of congratulatory messages. I know you'll really enjoy a couple. Here's one. 'Congratulations on the dedication of your new church. May God bless you and your wonderful work. Love from all of us. Church of the Beloved Disciple. Father Bob Clemens, New York.'

"And this one will knock you all right out of the back of the house. 'I regret prior commitments, March the seventh, will prevent my joining you for the dedication services of your new church building. Best wishes on this special occasion. Ronald Reagan, Governor of the State of California.'

"He can't come to visit us, but I'll be visiting him on June, the twenty-fifth, in Sacramento. On that date I will hold a peaceable demonstration marching from San Francisco to the capital in Sacramento, to protest against the antiquated sex laws.

"Now, there's one other person that I want to introduce. I want you to pick up an April issue of *Playboy*. This person is sort of, well, when you meet her, you wonder how she really made *Playboy*. But we're thrilled to death to have the woman who chaired the National Task Force on Homosexuality for the National Institute of Mental Health, Dr. Evelyn Hooker. Dr. Hooker, stand up and let us meet you. God bless you real, real good."

What a sensation. She receives a standing ovation, and I've never heard anything like it. I just go on saying, "God bless you." The congregation goes on with its ovation, with the sounds of "amens" sprinkled through it all, and with calls and whistles of appreciation. It just won't stop, and it is richly deserved.

"Dr. Hooker, come up here. Come up here!"

She comes to the podium and says, "It's awfully nice to be here." And even this simple statement is greeted with another round of applause. This woman is so charming and so warm and so bright that if she started reading the telephone book it would bring the house down. As she says, "Thank you very much," in acknowledging the love this congregation has for her, the Reverend John Hose steps up and we hear him interject this, over our shoulders, "You know every segment of society has a folk hero, and this is ours." And the statement prompts another wave of applause.

I say to Dr. Hooker, "Wouldn't you like to say something?"

She replies, "I want to wish you every success in this necessary and worthy undertaking."

"All right, God bless you. Isn't Jesus wonderful?" Dr. Hooker is ushered to her seat. There is more applause and more "amens."

"I want to introduce again our chancel choir . . . but just a minute, I want to tell you that I've just seen one other person, my former neighbor. She is a very interesting woman. She had three sons that Willie Smith was interested in. And she caught on. She watched Willie. And we all respected her, and we grew to love her. Marianne Johnston, wave at everybody. God bless your heart, Marianne. Praise the Lord. And especially because if it hadn't been for Marianne, I wouldn't be alive to be here today. God bless her real, real good.

"The main thing, is that we have all triumphed. And we're all here today rejoicing, and enjoying the certain knowledge that we have all come this far, at least."

Then I do introduce the choir. It does sing nicely. I open my prayer and scripture reading to begin my sermon. I ask the congregation to please be seated.

"David, I think, declared my sentiments completely when he said, 'I'd rather be a doorkeeper in the House of the Lord, than to be in the tent of the wicked.' Almost four thousand years ago, a very famous man built a very famous temple. We read in the scriptures that our chairman of deacons read to us this morning about when Solomon dedicated a church that his father had wished to have built. As I look at the story of MCC, and I think of our history and of the things that have transpired, I definitely see some comparison to David.

"David was king of Israel. More than anything in the world, he wanted to build God a House. But God would never permit him to do it. And I want to tell you, in our two years and four months of wandering, I've worried a little bit. And I kept thinking will we ever get in anything, oh, God, that we can call a House, that we can call Your House, the House of Prayer? And, finally, I thought, well, Lord, if You're not going to let me build it, maybe You'll let Papa John or one of the other ministers or Elder Lou or Reverend Richard Ploen, someone in the church, see that something would transpire—even if it didn't happen in my lifetime.

"Well, I look at that story of David, and I think of after Solomon built the Temple; something happened. All of the people got together. And they moved into the House of God. And when they got there and sung praises and hymns to the Lord, all at once the Spirit of the Lord moved into that Temple. And, when it did, a cloud descended onto the congregation. And the Spirit of the Lord was so strong in that place that the ministers couldn't even get up and minister because God was there. That's the way I feel this morning.

"I look back to October the sixth, 1968. I ran into some of the people who were at that first service. They're here this morning. I said, 'Well, what do you think?'

"And that couple said, 'We can't get seats.'

"I look back to that little group of Christians that met and prayed and *believed* that God could do a thing. It was something unusual and different that a group of persons would have to meet together just because of their sexual orientation. And yet, that's what it boiled down to. They were a group of people who felt that they were *denied* the right given to most Christians to even worship God. As I always say, in that service God moved! And when we got through, it wasn't a matter of having twelve or twelve hundred; we knew that the Spirit of the Lord had been in that service.

"Well, we started growing, and finally we reached the grand number of thirty-six. We just couldn't get 'em in the living room of my house anymore. And we said, 'We've gotta' find something.' You've heard that story, but I want to tell you something! A building does not make a church. We've got a church building here, but I want to tell you, if we get so wrapped up in this building and unwrapped in God we'll fail, like so many other churches have. If we get to the point where we forget *Him,* and we remember just ourselves, and we put us on the pedestal, and we say look what we've done, and we forget it was God who did it, for us, we'll fail! The day that we refuse to worship *God* and to serve *Him* and to look to *Him* as the author and finisher, we'll fail!

"But, if we look to *Him,* and we're the doorkeeper in the House of the Lord, we shall overcome. And we shall run the race with patience. And we shall see the end of this thing. Some people look at us and say, 'Oh, we're here. This is it.' But I want to tell you something, we've just begun."

As before, those shouts of "amen" reverberate through this room; they give me strength, and sustain and inspire me.

"This is just the start of this church. We're not going to give up and throw up our hands! We're not going to quit tomorrow! We're going to look to Jesus Christ! And we shall march forward victorious! With *Him!* Even after this Dedication Day. Amen."

And, again those enthusiastic "amens" roll back in chorus.

"Sometimes we become complacent. We think, oh goodness look at us, we have a thousand people here this morning. Look what we've done. We haven't done anything! To God be this glory! For ever and ever! Amen."

As the choir sings "God Cares," I sit in quiet meditation. We are about to ordain Elder Lou Lindsey a minister in this church. We are also to finally dedicate this big barn of a place that we have converted in the past two months from a wrecked, decaying, cluttered shell of debris to a stark, spacious and grand edifice to the glory of God. We shall go into the Mass, that most sacred and solemn part of our service. And, finally, the pastoral and choral benedictions. I have such mixed feelings. I feel friendly, warm, and triumphant. I feel that I have left so much unsaid. There are so many people I wanted to thank for all of their help. There are so many I have grown to know as friends, to love as brothers and fellow worshipers. Their faces swim into view before me, and recede. True, they have followed me, but most important, they have been drawn to God. I truly believe that God can help us explore what has been the unknown world of the gay people. It is a world unknown to most people. It is one we gay people do not yet fully comprehend ourselves. Some of us still fear that needed exploration, but we must overcome the fear and hatred that still is pressed upon us from so many blind and bigoted people. Nevertheless, we find ourselves, all of us, all of the gay people together, walking those first feeble steps into the community of men. And we do that through this church, which points the way. That is my mission in this life. That is the mission of this church.

The service has ended. I hurry to my office to change after standing in the long receiving line. The throng just won't quit. It surges through the church. Groups form. They congratulate one another—and all so rightly so. There is a long line for coffee and cake being served in what will soon be the choir room, I hope. Our honored guests, dignitaries, friends come and press their best wishes upon us all, literally. I have a press interview. It is an endless parade which one doesn't want to end, for *this* day will not be repeated. Never! We all know that. Yes, we will worship in this building, but it will change. Today's spirit will grow into something else. How challenging is the unknown. I must come to grips with it. As always, I must rush forward to meet it!

Chapter Ten
Outreach

I did rush forward to meet the challenging unknown. In so doing, I have dared what no one else attempted, an outreach into the gay community—this world of the homosexual—and I have brought these attitudes to the conventional world, to the establishment. I have melded my own sexual orientation with an active, open philosophy of life. For me it works. I have seen it work very well for others. We are trying to make it work for all. To do so, we must open new horizons, new vistas, for everyone. Part of our mission is enlightenment and education. True, we begin with the homosexual's basic acceptance of himself. From there, we go to his relationships to others, to his community and most important of all, to his relationship with God. Those are urgent goals of the homosexual world. That is our heritage. Thus, where we can, we reshape essential human dignity. There are griefs, expectations and disappointments along the way. But the rewards are great. They are uplifting and soul satisfying.

Our outreach is not just geographic. It would be silly if it were. Our basic outreach is not only spiritual and religious, but also one of activist reform. We are a *nonviolent,* but aggressive organization determined to change laws that have been used against us. We insist on equal respect in the brotherhood of man.

What has happened here in Los Angeles, and elsewhere, is that we have made the Christopher Street West Parade an annual event. In 1971, it was a great success. We were not molested by the police. They did oversee traffic and public order. Tens of thousands turned out and lined the sidewalks. Others watched us on local television. We were covered on statewide radio news broadcasts as well as in published wire service and local news stories.

The 1972 parade promises to be greater, but how we'll top the floats, the exhibits, the enthusiasm, the marching musicians, and the organization of 1971's parade is something that I wonder about. Yet, I know the people in my congregation will compete to do just that.

Again, we have a sex reform bill before the legislature. Again, it is sponsored by Willie Brown of San Francisco. We shall campaign to have it passed. Last year it did come to a vote, and went down to defeat, but by a narrow margin.

In June of 1971, I marched with a small group of friends and faithful followers from San Francisco to Sacramento to dramatize the need for passage of the sexual freedom bill. I fasted for much of the march.

We set off on what we termed our "Long March" on Sunday, June 20th at 8:15 in the morning. The sky was overcast. I was afraid we'd be rained on the whole way, but that day it just stayed cloudy. We had, as our goal, a June 25th rally on the steps of the State Capitol Building in Sacramento. It was 110 long, weary miles away, but that first day we covered twenty-five miles. Most of us had blistered feet when we made camp in an orchard grove outside Walnut Creek. We had support vehicles. We followed our route and were escorted by sympathetic highway patrol officers, and from time to time, deputy sheriffs, who aided us in evading a film crew determined to use us in a motion picture.

We made about twenty miles a day. I have never been so tired, so hungry and so close to losing my temper so many times. Finally, I had to abandon my fast because of the heat of the Sacramento River Valley. That, and my doctor's orders, reminded me that reason was more prudent than resolve. I nearly lost my temper at that film crew. I was suspicious of deputies, until they advised me to have everyone keep his cool. They said that we'd kept it this long, why lose it now and provoke some incident.

At the capitol, we were addressed by Assemblyman Willie Brown and his colleague, John Burton, who thanked us for the demonstration, outlined plans for effective support of the bill, and urged us to continue our efforts. Then, a very strange happened. A halo appeared around the sun just as we asked for a sign from God that we were doing the right thing. Reverend Howard Wells summed it up when he said, "God has shown He is with us, and if God be with us, who can be against us?"

Why the march in the first place? Judge Mildred L. Lillie of the State Court of Appeal said, "The place to challenge sex laws is in the legislature rather than the courts." Our problem was that when we'd go to the legislature, they often said go to the courts; the courts, in turn, sent us to the legislature. It was one big runaround. We have to break the vicious circle. Both of them must talk to us. Both of them must be made to see how silly these archaic sex laws are.

On January 23, 1971, we held a rally in De Longpre Park in Hollywood. We then marched on the Hollywood Police Station on Wilcox Avenue. We carried signs. We marched. We chanted. We protested police brutality against the gay community. We asked for an end to harassment and discriminatory law enforcement.

I spoke in the park. This is part of what I said:

I like to run a meeting like this like it was a revival meeting. . . . This one is a Gay Power revival! We're going to show some of this power here today. As I've said so many times, we're not afraid any more! We're showing it by being in meetings like this, and by standing up and being counted. It's our right as citizens of this country.

I want to tell you something, we're not going to be oppressed any more.

We pledge allegiance to a flag that we say gives us the right as citizens of this country to freedom and justice for all. Well, I'm afraid that's a lie today for the gay community. We have to stand up and be counted. Let people know where we stand. We're not afraid anymore!

They can shoot us, they can beat our brothers to death, but I want to tell you something: They might destroy this body of mine, but they can't destroy my spirit. They can't stop me from going on.

They might destroy you. They might arrest you. They might put you in jail. But you remember this: You're gay and you're proud!

Others spoke. Some insisted that our Police Chief, Mr. Davis, was a member of the John Birch Society. Some carried signs that said, "STOP POLICE BRUTALITY AND ENTRAPMENT OF HOMOSEXUALS!", "PIGS SUCK IN CLOSETS!", "THE NORTH VIETNAMESE NEVER CALLED ME A QUEER!"

We were picketed by members of the National Socialist American Workers Party, all two of them, wearing their Nazi swastikas and carring signs advocating "WHITE POWER." We kept the sidewalks open and we kept moving.

There were less than three hundred of us, but we were united in our purpose.

We wanted no more cases of gay people showing up with

bruises, beaten bloody noses, or just quietly and effectively beaten bodies. That's what we were really fighting against.

Recently, I welcomed the opportunity to testify before the hearings conducted in Los Angeles by the Joint Legislative Committee for Revision of the Penal Code of the State of California. The hearings were in progress when I arrived with another friend, a leading activist in the gay civil rights movement who was also going to testify.

One witness was just leaving the stand and another was being sworn by State Assemblyman Alan Sieroty of Beverly Hills, who chaired the meetings.

We heard the testimony of the new witness. His testimony was incredible! Because the new penal code would legalize sex acts between consenting adults in private, this man was furious. I assumed that he was incensed because the changes in the laws might let the gays here live an easier, more honest and dignified life! He repeated that homosexuality was a disease, that it always lead to the downfall of a culture, and sweeping aside all evidence to the contrary, that all gay people are child molesters. (Actually, over eighty-five percent of child molestation cases are committed by heterosexuals.) He was shocked to have to say that it was not unusual for some homosexuals to have fifty or sixty sexual contacts in a month.

I couldn't believe my ears!

He went on to misquote Dr. Evelyn Hooker, a woman I highly respect, and then launched what I considered to be an all-out attack on Metropolitan Community Church. My blood was really boiling.

Finally this man ended his testimony. Assemblyman Sieroty thanked him and said, "We appreciate your testimony. We will have, I think, now a rebuttal to your testimony."

I was called, went to the witness stand, was sworn and began my testimony. This is what I said.

"I would like to proceed. I want to, of course, rebut what was said.

"I was very interested that the dear brother has never attended my church, so he doesn't know what the precepts of my church are as far as proselytizing, as he called it, other individuals into the church.

"In opening, I would like to state that my church was founded because homosexuals simply didn't have any other place to go. . . .

"I also heard Dr. Evelyn Hooker misquoted. Dr. Hooker is a personal friend of mine. She was the Chairwoman on the Task Force of Homosexuality for the National Institute of Mental Health. I also heard our dear doctor make a remark that there is a cure for homosexuality. I have read articles by many, many psychiatrists, sociologists and psychologists who have discussed the areas of homosexuality. There is probably a minority in America that feels homosexuality can be cured. They have yet to prove that it can be. This also includes the gentleman who just spoke. As far as homosexuals are concerned and as far as curing them, we say there is no cure. We base this on the research of Dr. Hooker and other psychologists and sociologists who have done research in this area.

Dr. Hooker stated in the Final Report of the Task Force on Homosexuality, which she headed for the National Institute of Mental Health in 1969, the following:

> With respect to change in homosexual orientation, the current literature suggests that perhaps one-fifth of those exclusively homosexual individuals who present themselves for treatment are enabled to achieve some heterosexual interests and competence if they are motivated to do so; that a much higher percentage (perhaps 50 percent) of predominantly homosexual persons having some heterosexual orientation and who present themselves for treatment can be helped to become predominantly heterosexual; but that in court-referred or parent-referred cases where motivation to change is

often lacking and cannot be engendered, treatment is much less successful.

"But, please note that she used the word 'helped.' She did not say 'cured.'

"Five states in this Union now have changed their laws relating to sexual behavior between consenting adults. The states of Colorado, Connecticut, Oregon, Iowa and Illinois. As far as I know, none of those states have slid into the ocean or none of them have stopped operating because they have adopted laws that pertain to sexual behavior between consenting adults.

"A problem in American society, and a problem in our society in California, is a problem of sexuality, not homosexuality. We become hysterical when we talk about the areas of sexuality. We become hysterical when we talk about sex education in schools, and yet we all perform sex in one form or another, unless we are celibate. . . .

"I am a member of a minority in this state, I am a homosexual; I am a criminal in this state by the very nature of my existence, or so some people interpret the laws that way. In this state homosexuals are arrested normally for lewd and lascivious conduct. As I read these Penal Code changes I noticed that the act of lewd and lascivious conduct has been removed from these. We are grateful for that.

"I am disturbed about another section; that is, section 910, and this is the one that I am going to address myself to. As the last speaker noted, we don't have legal homosexual marriages, we don't think. We are not sure about this. When our forefathers in their goodness developed the Constitution for the state of California and set up the marriage laws, they didn't think that the day would ever come when this would happen. Well, those days are here. Very honestly, there are homosexuals who want to marry. They have just as loving relationships as any other individuals do. They are workers. They work in government; they work for the state government, for the federal government, for the city government.

They are in every area of living, from school teaching to ditch digging. They are here, and it is a fact of life that we can't change that and we wouldn't want to.

"We hope that the state of California will come to realize this, too.

"In a straight bar in our community one of you gentlemen walks in and you are looking for a sex object and you see a woman sitting on a bar stool, you have had two or three drinks and you are interested in her, you would walk up to her and you would pinch her on her you-know-what and you would say, 'Hi, good-looking.' Now, she can do one of two things. She can turn around and slap you and say, 'Shove off, buddy,' or she can say, 'Hi.' If she says, 'Hi,' you can do one of two things. You can say 'Hi,' and walk on, or you can say, 'Hi, can I buy you a drink?' If you say, 'Hi, can I buy you a drink?' she can do one of two things. She can say, 'No,' or she can say, 'Yes,' If she says, 'Yes,' you are climbing up on that bar stool and you are going to buy her a drink, and a drink, and a drink and then you are going to say, 'My apartment is about three blocks from here. I have a bottle over there, so let's go have a drink.' She can do one of two things. She can say, 'No, I am not interested,' or she can say, 'Yes.' If she says, 'Yes,' you know you are going to have a good time.

"Now, I walk into a gay bar and I have a situation where one of you fellows is there and you turn me on and I presume that, because you are in a gay bar you are a homosexual, and I say, 'Hi, good-looking,' you may just turn out to be the LAPD who says, 'Hi.' Now that's discriminatory. They never send policewomen to sit around and wait for other males to offer drinks to them and arrest them in a straight bar. That is a horrible fallacy, and it is discriminatory enforcement of the law.

"In one breath the proposed penal code states that what adults do in private is all right, even though it is what is now called a "deviant" sexual act. But it becomes somewhat contradictory by prohibiting the means of an invitation to do so.

You can't ask or solicit for it. Experience demonstrates that this portion, section 910, would simply be used as another means of oppressing the gay community. It would be used against us, and only us!

"I had an interesting situation in my church. A member of my church had a friend who came here from San Francisco, California just visiting. He ended up in a situation where he was arrested in a gay bar, and supposedly charged with solicitation. This individual immediately called his friend. His friend said, 'I want to call the church. The church has attorneys that work in this area who are interested in helping you.' This man, of course, became very depressed. He was a school teacher. In the state of California automatically an arrest means a hearing, and he would lose his credential to teach. Well, the next morning they picked his body out of one of our lakes in this area. He had committed suicide. He couldn't stand to think of himself being arrested and having to go back and face the school board.

"Now, we contacted his school board, not because of his suicide and not to tell them he was a homosexual, but to find out what kind of teacher this man was. He had an excellent rating with that board. They couldn't understand why he committed suicide. They didn't know anything about the arrest. They just couldn't understand this. Personal friends, supposedly those who were his co-workers, didn't know, and they couldn't understand it. In fact, one of the remarks was, 'He was the best teacher in this school.'

"He had been driven to the brink of despair because of the active persecution by individuals such as the last speaker who has asked you to engage in it too. Isn't the persecution of homosexuals—and I want to close with this—like the persecution of the blacks in the South when, by virtue of the color of your skin you were a potential rapist and, therefore, you were not to have certain jobs, not to live in a certain area of town; you couldn't marry, you couldn't go to certain schools because of that? Doesn't it put those individuals in the same class with Adolf Eichmann, who had the real plan for taking care of the Jewish problem in Germany, just by exterminating them, destroying them?

"Homosexuality is not on the increase. The states, the countries that have changed their laws have not had an increase. Throughout history, with the exception of perhaps ancient Greece, the rate of homosexuality has been somewhere within four and ten percent. We are talking about homosexuals more and sexual behavior more, but our percentage hasn't risen. Many of us are just coming out of hiding. Yes, we are coming out and standing up, and we are gay, and we are proud of it. We don't have anything to be ashamed of, because we feel that we have something to contribute to this American society too."

Those who would have us conform must realize that conformity carries the seed of social petrification. It dehumanizes man. If the gay community is to really be accepted, it must avoid conformity to stereotype. Hostility, contempt and oppression have been the fundamental attitudes toward the homosexual, as expressed by every arm of government, and by almost every religious sect.

I call upon all churches to assume their responsibility to broaden horizons, challenge the status quo, and, when necessary, to alter social morality to enable God in Christ to work more effectively.

As I travel around this great country of ours, I meet more and more with heterosexuals who come out to hear me speak, who come to our meetings. They are concerned with the work we are doing. They find that we don't fit the image they previously held. Many of them become involved, actively, with our mission. I look forward to the day, when we will have an arm of the church—a mission—specifically to the heterosexual community. Ideally, it should start through other churches. It may happen sooner than a lot of people think.

Dr. Evelyn Hooker told us at our general conference in September of 1971 that she thought the work we did in counseling the troubled homosexuals was superior, and was fulfilling a great need in our community. "I thank God for this church," is what she said. She got an ovation for that, and it warmed my heart more than I can possibly explain.

Do I militantly seek other churches to stand with us? Yes! I most certainly do! I have sent them this letter, often published in our magazine and newsletters:

"I am not a creature from the outer darkness, as you seem to believe. I am a homosexual, and like most of the members of your Churches, a man of flesh and blood. I am a member of the Church . . . and an integral part of its people!

"I have a few things to say. Because I am not a diplomat, I do not have to mince words, nor do I have to please you or even persuade you. I owe you very little. You did not create this body; you do not live in it; you do not have to defend it when individuals try to destroy it; and I will not let you tell me what I can do with it!

"Because of my sexual orientation, you try to condemn me. For two thousand years I have watched you try to destroy my brothers and sisters. Many homosexuals have had trials of 'cruel mocking and scourging, yes, moreover, of bonds and imprisonment. They were stoned, they were cast asunder, were tempted, were slain with the sword; they wandered about in sheepskins and goatskins, being destitute, afflicted, tormented; people of whom the world was not worthy.'

"You have watched as we were placed on the rack, thrown to the flames, banished from the midst of society, and you have never said a word! Your heart cried out when, after almost four hundred years, you saw the plight of the black people in this country. When the water hoses, cattle prongs and dogs were used on black men, women and children, a muffled scream escaped your throats. At once your blind eyes opened to some of the social injustices around you. You marched with Dr. Martin Luther King in Birmingham, Washington, D. C., Selma and then that day in Memphis.

That terrible day in Memphis, your eyes became a fountain of tears. The mighty had fallen, and you wept!

"Sometimes you still weep, for the American Indians, for the Mexican Americans, and for the lonely child-soldiers . . . on both sides, that are dying in a dirty little war in Viet Nam.

"But what of the homosexuals? Did you weep when one was beaten to death by the police in Los Angeles? When another was shot in the back and killed in a park in Berkeley? And another imprisoned for life in Florida? Does it upset you that there are riots in New York . . . and that homosexuals demostrating for their rights in California are arrested for demanding their civil rights? If it does, you have not shown it. Jesus said, 'I know thy works, that thou art neither cold nor hot. I would thou wert cold or hot. So then because thou art lukewarm, and neither cold nor hot, I will spew thee out of my mouth.'

"Oh! Church, if only you would keep the teachings that were delieved to you . . . 'Love the Lord thy God with all your heart, mind, strength, and your neighbor as yourself. ' . . . But you haven't. You have rejected the homosexual . . . and now . . . for the most part he has rejected you!

"I am thankful that I still have a God. You cannot take Him away from me! He is the Author and Finisher of my Faith. His name is spelled LOVE! L O V E!!!!

"Church . . . if you will not let me worship Him in your Temples, I will worship Him in the Cathedral of my heart, and build for Him a Temple where others can worship with me.

"Church . . . it is you that left me, not I who left you. You would try to make me believe that He does not care for me, but I know; 'though I walk through the valley of the shadow of death, I will fear no evil; for thou art with me!'

"Oh! Bride of Christ! I pray that you will wake up and call ALL of your CHILDREN back to your bosom and soul. Back home to family and friends and loved ones. Church, only you can make that possible!"

That letter has gone out over my signature to a lot of people and places. It is true! The church will have to stop oppressing us. I mean every sect, every parish, every congregation, every synagogue, and anywhere that people meet to worship. Why? Because organized religion is the source of the most vicious oppression of the homosexuals throughout history; and especially in this country. It will change and ease the attitude in whole communities when churches can honestly change their stands pertaining to homosexual behavior in America, and I hope elsewhere, too.

If every church in America changed its policy regarding gay people, tomorrow, half of our battle would be won. It would surely make people stop and think. But it wouldn't make an automatic, overnight change. At this point in history, in America, the gay minority is the only minority left that you can honestly still get away with hating in public. The established churches could help. It would be wise for them to try to erase some of the bigotry that still works against us. It is like the bigotry and hatred against races and other minorities. It is deeply engrained. If I were to introduce a black friend of mine to some people in this country, America, even if he had a Ph.D., he would still be reviled as a "nigger," and to those persons I would still be a queer. But a vast majority of America would become agitated and concerned if their local pastor was involved in the Gay Liberation Movement. Until those pastors do become involved, *we will* continue!

I have been told by my brothers and sisters who are involved in the ministry of Roman Catholic and Protestant churches, "Yes, we believe that homosexuals can become a part of God's kingdom, but we don't believe there should be segregated churches for homosexuals."

Neither do I!

I think it must be a stench in the nostrils of God to know that in America there are "white" churches, "black" churches, "straight" churches, and so-called "gay" churches.

The only reason we have these gay churches in this country is the same reason that we have black churches. It's discrimination, pure and simple.

After the American War of Independence, slave was a key word for blacks. If a black slave was permitted in a church, it was a black church with a black minister. If a black was a "free man" he had to sit in the balcony or in a special segregated section of a white church—in the back of the building somewhere. Blacks were not permitted to become officers of the church, nor—God forbid—enter into the ministry. What was the natural reaction to that situation. Blacks started their own churches.

The same thing has taken place in the gay community. As gay people we are not permitted to enter the ministry of almost any religious denominations. Oh, yes, we can, in some instances, attend regular church services as long as we hide our sexual orientation.

I can hear the question now, "Why would anyone want to tell other people what they did in the privacy of his own bedroom?" We don't. But in America everyone *wants* to *know* what every other citizen does in his bedroom. The federal government wants to know, if I am going to have a security clearance, or if am to be drafted into the armed forces. If I seek a license to teach school or become a hairdresser, then the state government wants to know about my sex life. City governments insist on knowing about an individual's sexual orientation if he is going to dig ditches, collect garbage, or do anything else on the city payroll. *Everybody* wants to know what I do in *my* bedroom, and that includes churches. So, if I were to hypocritically date the deacon's single daughter in most churches, and pretend to be something I'm not, then I would be acceptable.

The Universal Fellowship of Metropolitan Community Churches was founded so gays would have a place to worship God in dignity, and not as lepers or outcasts, but as His creation, as His children. Some day we may be a part of the whole community, if as gay people, that is what we really want. Until then our church grows , doubling our numbers each year.

Now we number into the thousands of active members. We are open to all, gay and straight, black and white, and whatever. Many come to worship, some to seek faith, some to renew it, some to discover it for the first time, some to rediscover. It is never easy. From those who come, we marshal the troops for our campaigns for our rights. Those campaigns are our crusade, our mission, and we've just begun.

Where would you come to meet us? At the Metropolitan Community Church in any one of the following cities: Atlanta, Georgia; Chicago, Illinois; Costa Mesa, California; Dallas, Texas; Denver, Colorado; Fort Lauderdale, Florida; Fresno, California; Honolulu, Hawaii; Long Beach, California; Los Angeles, California; Miami, Florida; Milwaukee, Wisconsin; New Orleans, Louisiana; New York City, New York; Oakland, California; Oklahoma City, Oklahoma; Philadelphia, Pennsylvania, Phoenix, Arizona; Portland, Oregon; Riverside, Sacramento, San Diego, San Francisco, and San Jose, California; Tampa, Florida; Tucson, Arizona; Washington, D.C. The way we're growing, there just might be one in your own home town. Ask!

We are also expanding into such diverse places as Australia, New Zealand, Canada, Germany, England, Japan, India, the Philippines, Malaysia, Singapore, Israel, France, Italy, Switzerland, Austria, the Low Countries, various Baltic and Balkan States and into Latin America.

What stops us! Nothing, really. We're on our way.

Now I know some ask, but what of you, and what of those who were with you at the beginning? Well, I haven't seen Daniel, my first homosexual experience, for a long time. I did see him when I was visiting in Florida after my discharge from military service. And we had a high old time. But I haven't seen him since the church got under way.

Benny and I are friends—friends in the truly Puritan and platonic meaning of the word. I pray for his happiness and his continued success. He comes occasionally to church.

But what of Carlos whose arrest triggered the start of this church? He would be astonished to see the long chain reaction that his arrest had on the gay community and the gay movement in this country. Perhaps he is aware of it. I don't know. Carlos dropped from sight over three years ago. No one I know has seen or heard of or heard from him since. Carlos has vanished. But we all hope it's only temporary. Should he come to any service in any church in our denomination, his welcome would equal that given to the prodigal.

Epilogue

What of tomorrow? What does the future hold for me? What does it hold for my mission in this life? Who but God can foresee the future? No one. How much of the future is foreseeable by man? Five minutes? Five months? Five years? No, none of it. Yet, I am not dismayed. I am always the complete optimist. It is my optimism that has carried me, to this point. Optimism is a gift from God; it comes through faith in Him. That is how I came through the deserts of despair and loneliness. That optimism is the means whereby I was able to find myself. It gave me the strength and the fortitude to triumph over hatred, fear, ignorance, bigotry, stupidity, and oppression. God's gift of optimism brought me to the oasis of my own acceptance of myself, to the oasis of faith, to a constantly replenishing spiritual renewal, to an absolute trust in God and in His infinite mercies.

I see obtainable goals ahead for all of us. The effects of

what I started with Metropolitan Community Church are observable throughout the land. That spirit of emerging comradeship is reflected and echoed as other denominations begin to examine their own doctrine, and realize that they must make an accommodation with the gay members of their congregations. Such a move is still an all too feeble step.

I see us becoming a potent political force. In America we are changing political attitudes. Candidates for public office now actively seek our help and our endorsement. Members of my congregation join with other gay groups and become actively involved in political campaigns working on issues and giving time and effort to help elect candidates whose attitudes about us are changing. We have begun voter registration drives in the gay community. We lobby in local units of government, in state legislatures, and in Washington. We picket. We march. We demonstrate. Yes, now we are beginning to feel our own political muscle, and to show it where it counts. At long last, even gay people are running as known gays for public office.

But ahead of us lies a long, difficult battle. We must fight on the executive level, from the president on down, to change orders discriminating so disastrously against the gay men and women in the armed forces and in all areas of federal employment. We have to do the same thing on state and county levels, and in the cities. We have to battle for our rights in courts to change laws, and to revise the administration of justice so that we, too, can share in equal justice before the law as *is supposed* to be guaranteed to us by the Constitution of the United States of America!

All of this requires a long, well planned system of battle fronts. We must be prepared to go again and again through the deserts of hatred and prejudice. It will take us through the valley of the shadows where we will again be put to the test of the fire of hatred, vengeance, ignorance, and threats of violence. I shall still read in the press, see on television, and hear on my radio that gay people are being hassled,

rousted, beaten, unjustly jailed, unjustly tried, unjustly convicted, unjustly thrown into prison. I shall go on learning
that many gay people are losing their jobs, their whole
sources of income, their entire means of making a career and
a living, only because they dare to risk the discovery of
being gay. I will continue to be horrified by the stories of
women that I counsel who have their children snatched from
their breasts and are declared unfit mothers because they
dare to say that *they are gay and they are proud!* I will be
revolted to learn that another gay person has been uselessly,
senselessly, brutally, and cold bloodedly killed just for being
gay. I shall be sickened to learn that extortion still victimizes
gay people. I shall walk through the fires with those who
fight being gay because they don't understand and don't
know what it is, with those who cannot accept it in themselves, and with those who are driven to brutal reactions
when they see it in others. I will pray for them. I shall pray
with all of them, and I will ask God's help that we may all
join in the fraternity of the human race and learn to live in
peaceable acceptance of each other, and to accommodate our
differences.

Then we shall have the freedom and the power to attain
the mountain peaks where the air is pure and clear and
winds of liberation are blowing towards the gay community
—to every gay person. Then, shall we too shout from the
mountain top—just as other oppressed people have done
down through the ages, as they have struggled—that we are
somebody and have a rightful place in the community of
love with all liberated people!

This is my dream. I shall come to the City of God, to His
Kingdom, knowing I shall be totally accepted as myself,
sharing my "being somebody" with all gay people everywhere. I dream of that time when all people who are gay, all
who are hiding it, will step forth *freely* into the light of truth,
total acceptance and understanding. I fervently dream and
pray for that time when there is an end to hiding, an end to
fear, an end to being victimized. I dream that we can all come

out of hiding, that we can all stand tall and walk with our heads held high, because we are gay and we are proud. We will throw our arms around each other's shoulders without any shame. We will laugh together, weep together, share together, and march together. There will be an end to fear! We *will* stand together! We will unite! We will all know that we are God's own creatures, that He loves us, that He created us, that He blesses us, that He's proud of us, that He cares for us! We will walk with Him! All of this, I know, will happen! Because we are not afraid any more!

Postscript
by Charles Lucas

I am often asked how this book came about. Personal friends are curious to know how I became so deeply involved with it. Now is the moment to reveal the countless hours of taped interviews, the meetings, the editing, and all the onerous work that goes to bringing out a book. That's not the way it happened in this instance. There were interviews, observation, and a large amount of detective work prompted by my own vast ignorance of what had really been happening in sex and morals in the United States during the 1960s.

During most of that decade I lived almost continuously in Mexico. My return to California was prompted by the urgent need for intensive long-term voice therapy. My mute state required my abandoning a successful career in the performing arts and as a professor. My one advantage was having missed the upheaval in manners and morals. I could bring a certain naive objectivity to bear upon the events of the dizzying decade. But my first articles dealt with subjects that were closer to me. I wrote about Mexican history and culture, and the experience of living in Latin America. Happily one editor suggested that my rather scholarly approach might be ideal for dealing with the American scene.

I worked my way into it rather slowly. First I surveyed the underground press. This lead to all kinds of antiestablishment groups, sexual revolution, women's lib, and the homosexual revolution. As I regained my voice, my interviewing capacity took a more usual turn.

My appointment for an interview with Troy Perry was made on a Friday for the following Tuesday. On the intervening Sunday, I seized the opportunity to attend service with the congregation at the Encore Theatre at Melrose and Van Ness in Hollywood. I wanted to see the man in action.

Greeters welcome all who enter, and pass the ingoing crowd to busy ushers. The service ranged from the hilarious to the deeply moving. Pastor Troy Perry is a platform performer of the first rank. His hold over an audience is hypnotic. Here was a born leader with a dedication to his mission. Here before his congregation stood a showman out of the same mold as the pulpit greats of the past such as Aimee Semple McPherson and Billy Sunday. Energy flowed from Troy Perry and ignited his entire congregation.

As I sat in the incongruous setting of a rather starkly decorated neighborhood motion picture house, I first thought that this must be simply a parody of the Bible Belt services that take place in thousands of churches designed for the exclusively heterosexual sinners. But topical references to current events in the gay community, and gay jokes and references changed the picture. We moved from the sublime to the hilarious. But the sermon, and later the communion service, so obviously answered a deep spiritual need for the "lost gays," that I was touched by the poignance of the ceremony and the intensity of emotional feeling of uplift and love and peace that the rite engendered.

Whatever Troy Perry was up to, he was answering the

long neglected needs of the homosexual community. He also drew a number of sympathetic heterosexuals who were caught up by his mission.

The initial interview in his office was a rather rambling and free-wheeling one. There were countless interruptions. We finally adjourned to a lunch that we hoped would be free of interruptions. It wasn't.

When we concluded I asked for another interview. I also broached the subject of an autobiography or some kind of personal memoir. Troy was interested, but he explained that he did not have either the time or the inclination to attempt the job. I asked for and was granted permission to pursue the subject. I gave him copies of my published work and left.

With that Troy Perry and I were off on what has proved to be, for me, a most enlightening adventure. Troy said, "I'm not an intellectual, and I have no literary pretension, I've tried to write down some of my thoughts. But writing doesn't come to me, so I'll wait. Maybe the two of us can work something out." Lengthy or frequent interviews became impossible as his schedule became more overburdened. He is not a patient man. Often I had extremely sketchy material to work on. The rest I pieced out from other sources. Others I interviewed were happy to cooperate. Sometimes I had to abandon the project for other assignments.

Occasionally I was discouraged by the difficulty of capturing the dynamic personality of Troy Perry in print, and having him spring to life from the printed page as he does in person. To the degree that this book is successful, I must personally thank many people who have made this book possible.

Foremost is Troy's mother, Mrs. Edith Allen Perry. She is one of the most charming, warm-hearted people I have ever met. Her genuine selfless concern for others is inspiring. So is her own experience with the homosexual community.

I cannot adequately thank all of the others for their part in making this book a reality. But I must acknowledge the enthusiastic, patient help and support I got from Don Shepherd and Caroline McCoy, both of whom are—luckily for me—my agents.

My personal thanks are also due to Sylvia Cross, W. R. Turner, Richard W. Fisher, Alan de Witt, Geraldine Morris, King and Rachel Moody, Darío Santiago, Flora Mock, Nina Blanchard, Julia Shuman, Michael and Honeya Barth, Jo Chamberlin, and Herb Pomeroy all of whom contributed to the successful gestation period the book required.

Working with Troy was a delight. We have developed a firm friendship. Through the work with him I was able to actively enter into and study the social action arm of his church. It was a personally rewarding experience for me to man the phones at the MCC Crisis Intervention Center, to be trained and to work as a counselor in the Personal Services section, and to be subsequently trained as a Clinical Associate at the Los Angeles Suicide Prevention Center. In turn, that training and experience led me to help initiate a group called "Survivors Anonymous" at Metropolitan Community Church. It is one of the first chapters in what we hope will be an international movement to deal effectively with suicide.

I am proud to serve with the members of the Metropolitan Community Church congregations, and to stand with them in their cause. Most humbly I thank all of them.

Los Angeles, California
March 1972